Smart Is The New Gangster

by
DAVID DIPOALI

Without limiting the rights under the copyright reserved above, no part of this publication may be produced or transmitted in any form or by any means, whether electronical, mechanical photocopying, recording, storage retrieval systems, and or by any other means known, unknown and or created in the future, without the prior written consent of the publisher of this book.

Copyright © 2014 by Kaleidoscopic Publishing. All Rights Reserved.
ISBN - 978-0-9903853-6-3 (print)
ISBN - 978-0-9903853-7-0 (ebook)
ISBN - 978-0-9903853-8-7 (MOBI)
First published in 2014 by Kaleidoscopic Publishing
First Printing date for November 1, 2014
Printed in The United States

Library of Congress Cataloging-in-publication data
The name Kaleidoscopic and its symbol are trademarks of Kaleidoscopic Publishing

If you suspect that an unauthorized vendor or person is selling or distributing this publication, please contact us at www.kaleidoscopicpublishing.com You could be entitled to an award and remain anonymous for your reporting. This also applies to unauthorized copying and distributing.

CONTENTS

CHAPTER 1
BUILDING A MEAN TEAM 12
- Attorney 12
- What You need to know about your legal representation 14
- Secretary 18
- Treasurer 19
- Personal Manager 20
- Agent 21
- Hiring Assistants and other Help 23

CHAPTER 2
RUNNING YOUR OWN LABEL 28
- 360° Rights 29
- Masters 30
- College and Radio Station Searches 31
- Entourage 33
- Security 33
- Office Necessities 34
- Social Pages 34
- Website 34
- Digital Downloads 35
- Copyright 36
- Trademarks 37
- Domain Names 37
- Producers 38
- Mixers 39
- Songwriters 39
- Studio 40
- Artist 40

CHAPTER 3
CONTRACT/AGREEMENTS 41
    360° Terms 42
    Term 43
    Exclusivity 43
    Work For Hire 43
    Cross Collateralization 44
    Promotional and Free Goods 44
    Liquidation 45
    Accounting and objection 45
    Side Letter Clause 45
    All-In Deal 46
    Conduct 46
    Breach of Contract 46
    Non Partnership 46
    Indemnity and Covenant Not To Sue 47
    Jurisdiction 47
    Free Will 47
    Privacy 47
    Control 48
    Gross and Net receipts 49
    Pro Rata 49
    Life Insurance Policy 49
    Technically and Commercially Satisfying 50
    OTHER IMPORTANT NOTICES 51

CHAPTER 4
HOW CERTAIN PAYS ARE DETERMINED 53
    360° Deal Contracts 53
    Artist Determination 54
    Advances 54
    Royalties 55
    Escalations 55
    Foreign Royalties 56

At-Source	57
Tour Royalties	57
Digital Downloads	57
Reserves Against Returns	58
Producers	58
Producer Level	59
Advances	59
Royalties	59
Escalations	59
Foreign Royalties	60
Digital Downloads	60
Reserves Against Returns	60
Mixers	61
Songwriters	61
Songwriter Determination	62
Royalty Determinations	62
Advances	62
Reserves	63
Recording Industry Determination	63

CHAPTER 5
BOOK YOUR OWN SHOWS/EVENTS	64
Booking Calls to Promoters	65
You Have to Know Something about Your Venue	65
Rent Your Own Venues	68
How to Get Around Liquor Licenses	70

CHAPTER 6
SCHEDULE YOUR OWN TOURING	71
Key Representatives	71
Booking Agent	71
Touring Manager	72
Production Manager	72
Publicist	73

Merchandise Manager *73*
When and Where to Tour *73*
Budgeting *74*
Promoting the Event *76*
Launching the Tour *77*

CHAPTER 7
HOW TO BE YOUR OWN PUBLICIST 78

CHAPTER 8
SELLING YOUR OWN MERCHANDISE 81

CHAPTER 9
SHOOT YOUR OWN MUSIC VIDEOS 84

CHAPTER 10
SECURING ENTERTAINMENT VISAS FOR YOUR ARTISTS 87

CHAPTER 11
NEGOTIATING YOUR OWN FILM, SIT COM, REALITY SHOW, COMMERCIAL, AND SOUNDTRACK ALBUM DEALS 90
   Motion Pictures *90*
   Fees *91*
   Credits *92*
   Crawls *92*
      Main Title Songs *92*
      Single Card Credit *92*
      Score (underscore) *93*
      Kickers *93*
      Pay or Play *93*
      Sequels *93*
      Trailers *93*
      Billing Block *93*
      Trade Ads *94*
      Delivery Date *94*

Exclusivity *94*
Term *94*
Non Exclusive *94*
Spotting *94*
Final Cut (final assembly) *94*
Hold back Period *94*
Certificate of Authorship (coa) *95*
Commercials *95*

CHAPTER 12
HOW TO BE YOUR OWN PUBLISHER 97
    Music Publishing *98*
    Mechanical Royalties *98*
    Statutory Rate Per Song (per mechanical Royalties) *99*
    Performance Publishing Income) *100*
        Performance Rights Societies *100*
        Blanket Licenses *101*
    Other Publishing Income *101*
        Print Music *101*
        Synchronization and Transcription License *102*
        Foreign Subpublishing *102*
        Subpublisher's Fees *103*
        Foreign Printed Music *103*
    Administrator's Publishing Contract/Agreement *104*
    Other Publishings *107*
        Hood Novels and other Book Publishing *108*
        Cover Design....Judging a Book By its Cover *108*
        Cover Fonts *109*
        Distribution Deal *110*
    Magazine Publishing *112*
    Poetry and Quote Publishing *112*
    Screenplay Publishing *113*
    Pictorial Publishing *114*

CHAPTER 13
SECURING YOUR OWN BAR CODES AND ISBN NUMBERS...... 115

CHAPTER 14
SOLICIT YOUR OWN SPONSORS.. 119

CHAPTER 15
ETHICS 130

CHAPTER 16
BEING CREATIVE 131

CHAPTER 17
BEING YOUR OWN ARTIST 133

CHAPTER 18
MONEY AVENUES.. 138

LIMIT OF LIABILITY/DISCLAIMER OF WARRANTY

While the publisher and author have used their best efforts in preparing this book, they make no representations or warranties with respect to the accuracy or completeness of it; and specifically disclaim any implied warranties of merchantability or fitness for a particular purpose. No warranty may be created or extended by sales representatives or written sales materials. The advice and strategies contained herein may not be suitable for your situation. The publisher nor author is not engaged in rendering professional services, and you should consult a professional where professional advice is needed. Neither the publisher nor author shall be liable for any loss or profit or any other commercial damages, including but not limited to special, incidental, consequential, or other.

In addition, the Representations in this book change over time; and by necessity of the lapse in time between the writing and printing hereof, may possibly be out of date upon the First publication. Therefore, each reader must use caution in applying any material contained herein.

ACKNOWLEDGEMENTS

A great deal of work goes into the preparation of a completed book; and alot of people are due many thanks for their insight, experience, knowledge, patience, support, inspiration, and assistance.

You appreciate their efforts and greatly acknowledge them during the process. But have you ever contemplated those authors whom gives thanks to themselves? Even during award shows like the Screen Actor's Guild Awards (SGA), The Grammys, The Oscars, and etc., few people ever take the time to appreciate themselves. Its always their managers, stylists, wardrobe assistants, directors, producers, makeup artists, etc.

So here, I want to take the time to honor, whatever higher power that exists, in keeping me grounded and steadfast to completion of all three of my books. And to that, I'd like to give myself a pat on the back and say....You're listening to who made me rich.

Good Looking Out..................

INTRODUCTION

Running your own label or entertainment company isn't as complicated as it may appear. The most important thing you need to know is how to properly structure the company. One of my other publications, "Million Dollar Game" is my best recommendation for assisting you in choosing between the best business structures for the type of company you are trying to establish; and how to format that business in the most legitimate fashion to conduct your business operations through. It also informs on the subjects of securing business loans and obtaining business credit, something that is extremely resourceful when starting out.

    You'll also need various contracts, that are both modern and fair to your artists, employees, assistants and any further help that may further your business career. For this, I highly recommend that you purchase my other book, "X Marks The Spot." In it you'll find a variety of contracts from signing artists to hiring employees and independent contractors. Not to mention other contracts such as sponsorship proposals, talent management, publisher, personal managers, booking, distribution and other contractual agreements. Everything else not mentioned in either of those books are found herein this one. With that said, pay close attention because you're entering a whole new field. One that is grimy, one that is conniving, and one that has no mercy for those whom DO NOT READ THE FINE PRINT. But if you respect it and appreciate it as you go, Space would be your limit, because the sky would be too low.

    Well student, what are you waiting for? Take off....and take care.

BUILDING A MEAN TEAM

Building a mean team will make the difference in whether you become successful or whether your label status hit Ground Zero. Without a mean team artists usually go double wood or hit Zirconium. So it's extremely important to build a team of the credentials outlined below:

1. Attorney
2. Business Manager
3. Secretary
4. Treasurer
5. Personal Manager
6. Agent

Lets take a look at each of them in dept:

Attorney

Attorneys, a/k/a lawyers, are a vital piece of your puzzle when building your team. The reason is because an entertainment attorney can accelerate a music label and or artist career much faster than the label owner him or herself, while acting as an independent. Its because of the attorney's previous networking and moonlighting Resume before you. They know the navigation of the rough seas ahead and they can guide you around the OTHER killer whales and Great Whites that began circling when they began to smell your blood success leaking into the deep blue below. The major players consisting of these "con artists" are always in Los Angeles, Nashville, New York and Atlanta.

A great deal of artists and label owners waste piles of money on their entertainment attorney due to ignorance. And when I say ignorance I mean 'not knowing.' Attorneys are almost always needed **ONLY** for reviewing, approving and or writing or rewriting contracts and deals. Therefore, I strongly suggest that you only deal with your attorney specifically regarding this (unless you're facing a lawsuit), and pay him accordingly when in such need. That way, you save piles of money that could go more towards the promotion of your company. And if he ever disvalues your attention, don't hesitate to move forward with another attorney, whom would love the opportunity to make the ends.

When selecting your entertainment attorney, always remember that everybody looks GREAT when they're selling themselves. Ask questions like, 'what do their fees consist of and what are they determined by; and other things like where would you fit into their schedule; what's their criteria of speaking with them directly verses their secretaries and other assistants.' Visit them, check resumes, inquire as to their relationship in the industry. Ask further questions like, 'are their clients privacy respected; what's their resolutions for conflicts of interest, etc.' Don't be afraid to clear these things up instead of when they arise. You have to bear in mind that if you plan on sticking with these people, they could most likely be representing your label's best interest for quite some time (without causing anger to their biggest money clients) **(more about them later).**

CONTENTS

And always be extremely aware of those attorneys whom promotes to you "truck-loads dreams of cash." Use realistic instincts....and listen to them. One thing is worthy of knowing: an attorney should **NEVER** manage an artist, or get any of an artists publishing and or royalties. Run fast when you hear a conversation leading onto that path.

What You Need To Know About Your Legal Representation

Don't get me wrong, attorneys can be very efficient, can procure a great deal of things that you can't secure and or procure on your own; and can really make things happen. In fact, if you're envisioning the successful career in the entertainment field then you should most definitely familiarize yourself with attorneys. Why? Okay say you don't have the appearance or lingual tongue to secure a building to rent, buy or utilize for a night. Well, an attorney can handle that for you with no problem; and more likely for cheaper. There's many advantages attorneys can be to you; and in such a regard, you have to be creative and think outside the box. Don't be afraid to ask your potential attorney if he or she can handle a specific task for you that you otherwise does not have the professional background, appearance, and or communication skills to carry out on your own. After all, they're in this business to make money by any means necessary, even when legal business is slow.

There are also other important things to know about attorneys that no one wants to speak on individually. Its like being afraid to call out the gays (no offense if you are, I was just using an example. No one has ever gotten out of this life alive, its yours, do you). And that is, that attorneys are no more than greedy bastards looking out for their own financial interests.

But don't for one second think that you can do anything about this, all I'm stressing is that you should be aware of this as your third eye is concerned. In hindsight, which in law is defined as hypothetical thinking, or what could possibly happen - you may need an attorney more than you think, because in some matters 'unsolicited' material (which is material not submitted by an attorney), is unacceptable.

In another hindsight however, you may believe that you're hiring the best attorney for the suitable job, but actually you're not. Its like organized crime, they're all members of an organization which have sworn to take an oath; and their first duty is to the court, the second is to officers of the court, and the third is to behemoth corporations, or those whom pay like them. This is why the definition of 'attorney' is one whom practice law, not represent it. They (attorneys) interpret it (the law) as they can get away with bending it; and in-turn, represent everyone but the client, unless of course the other party's not willing to break bread.

When an attorney is hired, he or she moonlights with another attorney from the other side (whom is usually an old school colleague or other individual through some previous deal); and likely discusses a favorable incentive for themselves, which results in persuading you to accept the less likely outcome as possible. And sometimes these same attorneys are affiliates of the behemoths and disguise themselves as non-affiliates; and there afterwards they pretend to be on your side until you soon find out that he or she was ineffective; and its too late to raise any concerns in a court about them.

But as stated earlier, there's really nothing you can do about it, just be sure that you get the best deals you're comfortable with, and this can sometimes be achieved by shopping with different attorneys for different tasks. Its like dealing with the lesser of two evils. But hey, you gotta deal. With knowing that, whatever deal you choose to settle with, then you need to be satisfied with it within. But always keep in the back of your head that lawyers aint s*@#! Keep whatever credit you'd like to give them to yourself, because you'll soon realize for yourself that they're "polite liars" and "charmed cobras."

Unfortunately, you have to deal with them. And even so, have everything explained to you in layman terms.

Business Manager

Another important person to hire is a business manager. The business manager is like Your eagle-eye of all of your business endeavors. Most literatures and publications confuses the business manager with the personal manager. The distinction however is quite clear. The business manager handles all aspects of your business, while the personal manager handles all aspects of your personal affairs.

When deciding business managers you should be extremely careful. I usually like to set up a 'check-off' list of what I like and dislike about what my potential business manager will and don't do, like:

1. What else do they do besides overseeing my business affairs; and keeping track of my finances;
2. What are their pay determined by;
3. How long do they contract with their clients;

4. Do they have experience and patience in my particular situation (of being an up-start label owner or artist);
5. What are their methods for securing all of monies in which you're entitled;
6. Do they have any international experience with securing all monies you're owed;
7. Do they inform and enlighten me on all tax duties;
8. Are they prohibited from being awarded any referral fees from innducing my decision to place my money in investments and other purchases;
9. Do they allow you to approve and endorse all of your checks;
10. Do they permit audits by you on occassions; and
11. Anything else which is so important that you can dream of and imagine.

Your business manager should just more than oversee your business affairs and keep track of your finances. He or she should genuinely have your best interest. In addition, their pay should be determined by what you actually get paid; and should be capped off at 10% of your gross income. Your argument is that you have a substantial payout to so many other people involved in your career.

Their contracts should allow you an option of at least 3 years; and It should state that if no work is found by the manager within a year's time then the manager should be relieved of his or her duties.

Your business manager should also have some experience in the music industry; and should particularly have enough patience to bare with your career as it progresses to stardom; and he or she should be capable of doing more than familarize him or herself of royalties and monies, but also be capable of enlightening their clients on all tax duties they're responsible for; In addition to securing all of your payments that you are due - from domestic and international publishing and royalties, to 'at-source' monies.

What a good business manager **WON'T DO** is dictate what their clients should invest and or place their money in. They simply provide the client with the best optimistic truth and allow the client to make the final determination and or decision. And as busy as you are perfecting your craft, a good business manager is always encouraging you to utilize options of auditing them, or inspecting all documents and records pertaining to the two of yall's relationship. They understand that its transparency that binds the loyalty between the the two of you.

While its true that you can't save a person from themselves, your business manager can do a dam good job hiding any tools and or weapons that may assist in your suicide. But....you'll be sure to find other weapons and tools necessary to complete the job - but they'll almost always have to be found elsewhere.

Secretary

Another viable person on your team is the secretary. **NEVER FORGET**....if your books aint right, your s*@# aint right. This person is so essential because he or she is the direct overseer of every document and receipt regarding your label. With intact organized files, you won't have the least problem with locating an important document, contract, agreement, receipt, license, permit, etc. So at any given moment he or she is called on for a specific piece of information -that was once issued and now needed. He or she is that essential link to timely putting that accurate piece of information into your realm, providing you a professional service and appearance, and leaving your business associates a lasting impression that you are as organized as you are about your business.

But this shouldn't be your secretary's only strength. A secretary must also be strong in all aspects of office administration, use of office equipment, reception, data entry, handling multi-line phone systems, scheduling appointments, timely complete all given assignments, train employees, have outstanding communication skills, possess computer expertise, maintain strict record keeping, professionalism, vision, be internationally friendly, be capable of delivering powerful strategies, lays cornerstones for future products, proficient in analyzing and streamlining product delivery systems to produce productivity, quality and efficiency.

This type of secretary lends value to your company, that is priceless. Just whatever U do....**DONT GET RELATIONALLY INVOLVED WITH THEM,** unless you were relationally involved from the start. Because if so, you'll tear this motherfu@%#* down as fast as you build it up.

Treasurer

This person here could be a certified CPA or simply your treasurer. Its extremely important to encourage a close friendship with this person and your business manager, simultaneously.

One thing you **DON'T WANT** though, is for the both of them to be either: the same person, or relationally involved with eachother. However, you **DO WANT** the both of them to be on good accords with eachother because it promotes transparency between all parties. When this is occuring, there's no need to question either of the parties intentions.

But your treasurer experience must be sort of extensive. He or she must be knowledgeable in preparing financial statements, developing quarterly reports, have a strong background in finance and accounting practices, must be experienced in quickbooks, ADP, payroll, ms word, excel, access, data entry and word perfect, must be knowledgeable in complex spreadsheets, measuring financial performance; and have an in-dept understanding of a wide range of financial tools.

At the outset of up-starting your label, you are more likely than not to need this type of in-dept credentials. Actually, your secretary can carry out nearly the same functions that is needed to keep close track of your finances. However the story goes, have someone filling this position. If you're anything like me, then you're a fool about your money. There's no literature that I can think of that can tell you the true story of a fool and money soon departing. Its because money needs a boss! Else it'll make someone else one.

Personal Manager

Your personal manager is someone sacred to you. It should be someone whom opinion you value greatly. This is the person whom will handle all of your personal affairs. This is the person that you can trust with all of your personal information.

I like to look at this person somewhat like your rolodex. They're your reminder of certain personal endeavors, while you're trying to keep up with your prefessional career; and all others thats likely to carry out the assistance in boasting you to stardom. Their fees are usually capped off at 5% and when I think of choosing one, I think of hiring someone whom I admire, and or whom can keep me in check. Someone whom I deeply respect. Someone whom NEVER tells me what I want to hear, but what I NEED to know.

This could be your wife, baby momma, baby daddy, momma, best friend, school mate, etc. Whomever it is, they must be serious about being chosen for this type of position. They must also have the patience to baby sit you when you've lost track on specific performances, whether they're agreements, appearances, meetings, auditions, and or appointments. So be sure to choose a great business oriented person of this sort.

Agent

When it comes to selecting your agent, it is very important to know that there is a difference between agents in the film business and agents in the music business.

Agents in the music business are typically involved in everything regarding music, like assuring that all booking of concerts, tours, songwritings, merchandising, sponsorships, and or anything else regarding the subject, but on a much higher level than your business manager.

Agents in the film business are major players in the industry itself, with almost an unlimited sphere of influence. These agents usually deal with everything regarding film, tv, commercials, etc. However, both is almost always represented by a Union, usually one of the four: American Federation of Musicians (AFM, mainly a union representing musicians); American Federation of Television and Radio Artists (AFTRA, mainly a Union representing vocalists and actors on live, taped and digitally recorded media); Screen Actors Guild (SAG, a union mainly representing film); and Actors Equity (AE, a union representing live stage performances). These Unions usually cap their registered agents asking pay at 10%; and only on jobs the agents actually secure for the artists and performers. Remember though, these agents NEVER get any of your monies from earnings other than what they secure on your behalf.

Something to know however, is that Unions only allow their registered agents to be represented by agents whom agree to the Union's restrictions. In such case, these agents will only be allowed to use contracts issued by the Unions themselves. The contracts normally consist of films, filmed tv, commercials, concerts, performances, etc. It is wise not to contract with agents longer than a year, or at best have stated an option to exit the contract at your discretion for every year afterwards in case your agent is not fulfilling their duties. That way, you should have no problem telling them to kick rocks if things are not up to your par.

Be inadditionally aware that you should **NEVER** allow the agent to represent you in all areas of your life. This eliminates your business and personal manager; and would not be to your advantage. In all, once you choose your agent, he or she will basically be interacting with your business manager. Except when you're needed by the agent in particular.

HIRING ASSISTANTS AND OTHER HELP

Keeping up with every aspect of the music business is a talent within itself Remember what I said earlier, no one person is an Island. Thats why its seldom that an artist will perfect both the creative aspect and the business aspect. Look at JZ, its a reason he don't put out music back to back. Look at Cash Money, Slim is the behind-the-scenes man working the business aspect and Baby is working the boss artist aspect.

Although its not impossible, its just challenging to do it all by your lonesome, its just too much multitasking. Especially when you're still learning yourself as you go. Me myself, Id rather learn as I go, and have fun at the same time - any day of the week, than to learn and be stressed out on whether or not I have things correct. Having fun is just one of the advantages that a good group of help can do for you.

Theres unaccountable amounts of trustworthy employees and independent contractors just waiting to be hired. However, just don't set out to hire anybody because you need someone to help you out. Choose those people whom believe in you and whom see your vision. Hiring or selecting the opposite will fold your company before you can get it recognized on paper. So while scouting your help, be sure that they are worthy of the position, and not because you love them or some other excuse. This is almost always to end in failure. I was in boy scout and the first thing they teach us is the 12 steps that a scout should be: trustworthy, loyal, helpful, friendly, courtesy, kind, obedient, cheerful, thrifty, brave, clean, relevant. So when I hire help, this is what I scan for, in addition to them being organized, having leadership skills, and good comprehension qualities. I throw any favorable agendas out of the window, because this is my business, and I want it around for as long as it will carry itself; and so it is my duty to operate it like one. Any conflicts of interest that didn't agree with me not hiring them is tuff luck. At the end of the day I still have my business, I've made some very wise decisions in the employees that I chose, and everything is running smoothly, which allows me to focus more on my craft.

So when hiring, keep in mind of the boyscout creed. I've also included some other important characteristics to take notice of. They are listed below as followed. In my search, I like to look for traits of:

1. Someone whom is organized;
2. Someone whom is efficient;
3. Someone whom has decisive leadership skills in all areas including employee recruitment and training;
4. Someone whom has great communication skills;
5. Someone whom is a great listener;
6. Someone whom is attentive;
7. Someone whom is familiar with marketing and promotions;
8. Someone whom have visionary problem solving skills with the ability of conceiving complex solutions;
9. Someone whom is an effective communicator to superiors;
10. Someone whom is committed to the growth and the success to the company;

11. Someone with the ability to execute damage control, has undivided focus and empowers a team to excel and make advanced quotas;

12. Someone whom have the ability to oversee management teams across a diverse range of busimess enterprises; and

13. Someone whom is capable of analyzing, streamlining and tracking product delivery systems domestically and internationally.

I guarantee you, that keeping the above in mind while hiring, and your business will run efficiently without interruption. Always remember though, that your first priority must be to value your employees. Providing nice compensations and benefits to them will encourage their work enthusiasms.

But back to the main point of focus. There's many other positions that are available to be filled, like office managers, social media officers, marketing and promotions employees, entourages, researchers, travel arrangers, mail and package carriers, etc. Whomever you decide to choose, be sure to hire someone that you feel comfortable delegating responsibility according to your plans, instructions and techniques regarding the running of your business.

So who are some of these people whom you may want to hire? Some, if not most, are family members, wives, companions, friends, etc. These are great people to assist you. However, sometimes you can't mix any business with pleasure. And as soon as you see it not working, or you not accomplishing what should have been accomplished in a short period of time - RUN! Don't hesitate with fooling yourself about something thats never going to change. it'll only get worse and you'll only regret not running earlier. And though it would be hard firing someone you love, or are jointly tied to, it has to be done when the circumstance calls for it. Its only tough love. No other job owner will allow them to get away with anything and you shouldn't either. On the other hand, if I would consider allowing someone to get away with something within my business, I'd rather it be someone I love and trust. But ultimately, you'll have to weigh your pros and cons.

College interns may be another area to look. Check around at your local Universities to inquire if students are interested. The hourly rates may be very reasonable; and the students benefit from the real work experience. But check your wage regulations to see exactly how intern students are to be paid. If I'm not mistaken, a new law says that they have to be paid a bare minimum.

In any event, find a freshman whom will be around for at least three to four semesters, and possibly during the summers. These people commit substantially to your career.

The last alternative is to advertise in the local arts and entertainment newspapers or your local classified sections. That has been proven to be very resourceful. As stated earlier, whatever you decide, always remember that good relationships are key to the rise of an empire. Remember, you don't know everything, you're simply trying to learn. So be attentive, recruit those smarter than you, don't be afraid or intimidated or prideful to learn. Listening is an art.

CONGRADULATIONS! you've done it! You've built a mean team. There's many advantage to having a well equipped one. Use them to your label's advantage. Listen to their outrageous ideas; and don't be afraid to implement those thinkings that appear outside of the box.

THEY SAY WITHIN THE SHADOW OF A GREAT KING OR QUEEN, STANDS A GREAT TEAM! Believe it!

II

RUNNING YOUR OWN LABEL

In this section I'll show you how to run your label and or entertainment company. The first misconception about It is that you have to have all this money. Not completely true. To the extent that you need some money, my other book "Million Dollar Game" will take you through the hush hushed steps of how to establish a company, give it an immediate $1,000,000 dollars in instant value and then secure a loan for approximately 65% of that million dollars to fund your company. If you don't believe me, then see for yourself. If you want it, then put in the work and read the book. What I won't be doing is giving you anything for free. I'm not good at having patience for convincing. Like alot of others would have it, its better kept a limited secret. That way it don't get abused by those that is undeserving.

But here, we'll be talking about everything you need and need to know about running the label. Things like the following:

1. 360 Rights;
2. Masters;
3. College and radio station searches;
4. Entourages;
5. Security;

6. Office Necessities;
7. Social Pages;
8. Websites;
9. Digital Downloads;
10. Copyrights;
11. Incorporate;
12. Trademark;
13. Domain Names;
14. Producer;
15. Mixer;
16. Songwriter;
17. Studio; and
18. Artist;

Lets address each of these in layman terms, starting with 360° Rights:

360° Rights

Almost every label contract out today, has a clause within it that lists a 360° Right relinquishment. What this particularly mean is that your label and or entertainment company will share in a portion of **ALL** monies to which its signed artists receive outside of music. Your label or entertainment company's argument is that they are taking on the role of building their artists, performers, entertainers, etc. into a household name, making him or her a brand, or at the minimum, a celebrity. So if income is coming in from other avenues outside of music, because of your status built by the label, then the label is entitled to a percentage of it.

Signing to a label or entertainment company that has 360° Rights in their contracts are impossible to escape. In fact, 99½% of all label owners will not sign you without you agreeing to such. However, the labels have legitimate concerns in their request of 360° Rights, which is a plus for you. They've figured that if you don't make it in the music industry and they've put all this money into and behind you, then its a strong possibility that you may make it in another field, like modeling, acting, sports, commentator, etc. And that they can recoup their investments and afford you another chance at making a living. So don't be all that concerned about 360° Rights. They're to your advantage.

Masters

A Master is the original recording from which all other copies are made. It is the final project of the instrumentals recorded on a separate track or channel, and the voice recorded on another track or channel. When both recordings are finished, they're edited, mixed and eq'd; and are mostly finalized on computer.

Music labels usually require the artists to deliver approximately 14 songs a period (which means a certain term, or year). The labels usually require the artists to relinquish the Masters to each of those songs. Their arguments are all the same, that they're investing in you and will need Rights to exploit every avenue available to recoup their monies. However, you as an artist should try your hand at negotiating to co-own the Masters with the label. I don't know if you will prevail, but its worth a try.

As a label owner, you should **NEVER** give up ownership of **ANY** Masters, it is your bread and butter for now and the future. Look at what the beetles and Michael Jackson catalogs became worth today.

College and Radio Station Searches

The next thing you wanna do is an internet search, locating **ALL** college and other radio stations in every major city within the United States. Once this is done, separate them in brackets. For example, one bracket should be strictly for college radio stations. Another should be for country, then rap, then r&b, pop, soft rock, alternative, etc. The searching of these stations should include online stations as well. Onced finished, do a search for all music and record stores within these major cities also; then divide them by their brackets too. Myself, when I started out, I searched for all clubs, hole-in-the-walls, and Djs. I would very much recommend you do this as well. This gives you the advantage of knowing where to send your music or make your world premiere performances.

Below I have supplied 25 power Djs and radio stations for you to include into your catalog, although they are for one genre of music:

1. Hot 97 (New York), FunkMaster Flex;
2. V-103 (Atlanta), Greg Street;
3. Power 105.1 (New York), The Breakfast Club;
4. WEDR (Miami), DJ Khaled;

5. Power 106 (Los Angeles), Big Boy's Neighborhood;
6. 92.3 Now (New york), Nick Cannon;
7. 93.9 WKYS (Washington, D.C.), DJ Quicksilva;
8. Hot 107.9 (Atlanta), Durrty Boyz;
9. The Box 97.9 (Houston), The Madd Hatta Morning Show;
10. 98 WJLB (Detroit), Bushman;
11. 94.1 (Savanna), The Ricky Smiley Show;
12. 93.1 (Savanna), The T-Roy Show;
13. 95.5 WPGC (Washington, D.C.), The Big Tigger Morning Show;
14. Power 99 (Philadelphia), The Hot Boyz;
15. 92Q (Baltimore), Konan;
16. Power 92 (Chicago), DJ Pharris;
17. K104 (Dallas), Bay Bay;
18. 106 KMEL (San Francisco), Big Von;
19. Hot 107.9 (Philadelphia), Kendra G;
20. 101.5 (Jacksonville, Florida), Tom Joyner;
21. Power 98 (Charlotte), No Limit Larry & The Morning Madhouse;
22. K975 (Raleigh, NO, Brian Dawson;
23. Q93 (New Orleans), Wild Wayne;
24. K97 (Memphis), Devin Steel;
25. Hot 104.1 (St. Louis), Staci Static;

There's other big name DJs, out there as well, like DJ Clue from New York; DJ Felli Fel from Los Angeles; Angie Martinez from New York; Ryan Cameron from Atlanta, EZ Street from Washington, D.C.; and The Cipha Sound And Rosenberg Show.

You can find other known and unknown DJs in major cities by reading hip hop publications like Hip Hop Weekly, etc. So began your search now.

Entourage

Next you need to arm your label or yourself as an artist, with a walled entourage. This should consist of the prettiest, classiest, finest and gorgeous females, in addition to the hardest headed die hard crew (or what some would refer to them as....thugs).

This instantly builds and skyrockets your fan base, something you desperately need at this stage of establishing yourself or your label. However, there's things that you will need to acquire to give your entourage an credible and or professional look, as you move to stake your claim in the music industry. Those things are T-shirts, promotional walls, art canvases, wrapped vehicles, hand towels, caps, hoodies, flyers, banners, signages, Posters, brochures, etc. So be sure to purchase each of these things.

Security

A mandatory position you want to have occupied within your entourage is security, The look it gives your entourage sort of displays that you have a right to act hyphy. Security also gives the presence that your crew is a very popular group. This makes people interested in who you are, what genre of music you deliver and puts them on an inducement to listen out for your image and or music in stores and other media.

Office Necessities

Initially establishing yourself or your label, you're going to need some extremely important things for your office. These things gives the serious impression that you are operating on a real business level. With that said you're going to need a color printer, a fax and copy machine, business cards, envelopes, unglazed paper (usually in the size of 8x11½), stationary and embossed stamps, a computer, a rug bearing your logo and entertainment company name, and anything else that you can think of for the label's office.

Social Pages

This here, as everybody know, is a no-brainer. We all should know that you should establish a fb, twitter, and instagram page for your label, and those pages should have hyper links to your main website, so when you do postings, it'll immediately forward to your social pages, wherein all of your label followers and or fan base is alerted; and enticed to see what you have done or accomplished.

However, make sure the content you post about your label is clean, intelligently written and easy to understand. Your look should always be aimed at being professional.

Website

As a professional company that is taken seriously, your label should always have a clutter free, and easy to navigate website.

It must entails everything that the label does or intends to do. It should have a page for the postings of videos, interviews, bios, models, entourage, etc. It should list and post all events, concerts, backstage clippings, photos, meet and greets, behind the scenes, etc. This keeps people visiting your site, for the sake of following you; attending places you intend to be, when near their areas; and supporting your endeavors when you release them to the public. It is also very important to establish links to your site when you post pictures and content to other sites.

One final thing to remember is that your website's web address name, show up in the top rankings in search engines.

Digital Downloads

As a label owner or independent artist, you want to maximize every money avenue stream available. And in doing this, you're going to need to conduct another internet search. But this search will deal strictly in musical download companies. And when found, you wanna sign your label up with everyone from U-tube to soundcloud.

And please, most definitely sign your music up with those distributing companies that sells downloadable music to federal and state prisons, This is BIG BUSINESS! Everybody has cashed in on it, from telephone services providers to mp3 manufacturers. You may as well get your cut too. Below, I've listed some digital download websites that you can submit your music on to be sold:

1. Itunes.com
2. Amazon.com
3. Rhapsody.com

4. Napster.com

5. Android.com

6. Windowsmedia.com

7. Zune.net

8. Limewire.com

9. frostwire.com

10. e-music.com

11. Groupietunes.com

12. Laia.com

13. Shockhound.com

14. Digitaldownloader.com

15. Spotify.com

16. Soundcloud.com

I recommend that you visit these websites and understand their registering process, and their terms associated with publishing your music in digital format. In addition, there are hundreds (if not more) websites out there, other than the ones listed here. These are but a few.

Copyrights

Copyrights were designed to protect the property and rights of content written and authored by a person or group. So when your music is written down for the first time, register it with the Library of Congress as soon as possible. And although your work is not required to be copyrighted, its much safer to do so. For a greater understanding of copyrights, how it works and what its designed to protect, see my other publication called "Million Dollar Game."

Trademarks

Trademarks are just as important as copyrights. The difference between the two is that when trademarking you're protecting your company's logo. After all, it is the image and brand that you put so much blood sweat and years into. And the last thing you wanna do is have someone else water it down by using it without your permission; or using it totally unrelated to what you established it for. My publication "Million Dollar Game" also informs on the inns and outs of this topic as well.

Domain Names

Another important piece of the puzzle to owning and running your own label or being your own artist is to secure your label or user name's domain names.

A domain name is an internet web address (like www.musiclabel.com). Its how people pin point you when seeking you out on the internet. It provides a solid presence into your cyber world, as it regards informing on your label, artists, tours, merchandise, talents, events, pictures, etc. So this is very important.

For like $9.00 a year, you can own your own internet domain name. So don't be fooled by companies who charge you more. The top domain name provider today is www.1and1.com Its currently the AAA Top-of-the-line internet domain hoster and seller. Learn more about domain names in "Million Dollar game."

Producers

Producers are the first most valuable player on your label. Because they are the ones responsible for introducing the label or the artist, to that smash hit beat. But producers do more than make beats, they match artists with feature artists in the same genre, and they instruct artists to find their lows and highs, at just the right moments, when breathing on the tracks.

There are a number of websites that allows the public to use free beats from producers that only require an exchange for acknowledgements of the producers identity. You can also be your own producer if you're familiar with the craft. And you don't need a big, high price dollar studio to produce high quality beats. Always remember, you can iron out any unwanted sounds and tings in the mixing process.

Below is some names of the hottest producers in the game: Ariel Rechtshaid; Bangladesh; Beat Billionaire; Beats by the Pound; Benny Blanco; Cardiak; Childish Major; Cool & Dre; Da Internz; Dallas Austin; Detail; Diplo; DJ Diamond Kuts; DJ Mustard; DJ Scream; DJ Spinz; Doc McKinney; Don Vito; Easter Dean; Fisticliffs; Free School; FRI; Glass Da Boss; Happy Perez; Hit Boy; Illangelo; Jim Jonsin; Johnny Cabbell; J.U.S.T.I.C.E. League; Kane Beatz; Ke; Kenoe; Lex Lugar; Lifted; Manny Fresh; Mike Dean; Mike Will; Mr. Morris; Ms Shyneka; M16; NNikhil; Noah 40 Shebib; No i.d.; Otis Williams, jr.; Polow Da Don; Pop Oak; Pop and Oak; Redd Stylez; Rico Love; Ryan Tedder; Schife; Shama Joseph; Shanell Woodgett; Shawty Red; Shea Taylor; SI & Caleb; Sneak Beatz; Sonny Digital; Sound M.O.B.; Soundwave; Tha Bizness; The Invasion; The Lottery; The Renegades; The Runners; Tiara Thomas;

T-Minus; Troy Taylor; Warren G; Xavier Dotson; Young Fyre; Young Snead; Yung Ladd; and Zay Toven.

Mixers

The next person you want on your label team or behind you as an artist is a mixer. This person is alomst always confused with the producer, although you have some producers whom are mixers as well.

But a mixer is someone whom are capable of detecting out of chord sounds. They're given the gift to listen to what ranges are given a particular song, based on what mood the artist deliver it in. This is their job and what they're paid to detect.

But most, if not all of the time, a mixer completes the final editing process; and delivers the original Master to the label owner and or artist. This is what they're ultimately paid for.

Songwriters

Some artists are blessed with the talent to write and perform their own music, as well as choose correctly their own unique style of dressing and swaggering. But unfortunately, some artists may not. This is when you as the label owner or artist, enlist a team of ghostwriters. There's alot that the artist will have to keep minded of, like performances, lyrics, his or her particular choice of style, performance dates, a number of upcoming songs, in addition to things that go on in their daily lives like fame and the rest of personal family matters. I like to ease the burden on most of my artists until they've proven themselves. So what I do is have songwriters writing the lyrics and have the artist choose which of the songs that he or she ultimately like. This is helpful to both the label and the artist due to the fact that a songwriting team can keep the artist's lyrics modern, relevant and up to trend with slangs, etc.

Studio

I advised you earlier that you didn't need a studio to make good quality music, but it is however, a critical piece to the puzzle. Reason being is because it provides the label or artist a place wherein it could say that its conducting its business. If an artists constantly works from the studio in his or her garage or basement, at some point it stops becoming business and the artists usually lose interest. But when an artist constantly have to show up at a place called a music studio, then it actually encourages him or her to push forward. It includes them to feel as if though they're actually putting forth a sweat towards their dream.

The musical equipment thats needed to be purchased for a studio comes in many plans. It does not have to be purchased outright, it can be financed. And if you're really smart, you can have it pay for itself, by allocating studio time to be sold to the public. who knows, you may even find a hit artist in the process.

Artist

And finally, you can't have a label if you don't have an artist. Social media is just abuzzed with artists with social pages. And most of them have already done majority of the footwork, like already have experience in shooting their own videos, going on local tours, shooting independent film clips, producing and mixing and etc. Search all the social media platforms. Even Myspace is still a hot spot for talent of these sorts.

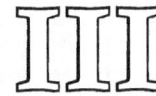

LABEL CONTRACTS

In this Chapter we'll discuss what should be included in your label's standard contracts. Although some situations are the same, not all are, and what I'm informing you on is only meant for you to use it as a guide on how you set various provisions that is beneficial to both you and your artists, and any other of your team players. Don't be sheisty, there's way more than enough money for everyone to eat, and for you to still be able to come out on top like a fat rat. In fact, a fair contract encourages talent and team players to push forward. The more money is made, the more they get paid. You can't do it without them, so treat them as you would want to be treated. They're your best investments; and you are theirs.

Contract/Agreements

A contract is very much so a hybrid of an agreement. It spells out certain terms within and the other party(s) agree to them. The contract/agreement can be structured in unlimited ways, depending on what's agreed to and what's the language stated within it. Contract manufacturers, and agreers alike can both, and each, be very creative when structuring contract/agreements. However, whatever stated in the contract and agreed to, you must be aware, as an artist or a label owner, that certain things cannot be omitted. Lets go through the most essential provisions that must be alleged:

360° Terms

360° Terms is listed within almost every contract today, from Major labels to independents. While signed to the label, or artist, they consist of the relinquish of your rights pursuant to 360° terms, under all avenues available that can generate income for the artist or label. It automatically consists of side work or additional work consisting of copyrights, trademarks, incorporations, businesses, Other Master Recordings, etc. and any and everything else associated with the Artist, his name, image and or likeness, such as films, videos, fashion, apparel lines, stand-up comedy, stand-up performances, documentaries, reality shows, commercials, trailers, sit coms, amateur videos (adult or otherwise), business ventures, touring, sponsorships, endorsements, song writing, previous written songs or lyrics that hasn't been used in any other recordings, sport activities, charities, video games, pictorials, theatricals, voice overs, voice tones, digital and non digital merchandise, side person performance, joint recordings, coupling, features, webcasting, streaming on demand, wifi, digital and non digital downloads, companies, and or any other gizmos or other technology not yet invented, not yet common and or unknown at this time; and or any other avenues that generate income for the label or artist, that is not yet invented, not yet common, and or unknown at this time.

Well, hope you get my drift. These people want their money if they invest in you. And they want their money if they could have invested in someone else, but instead missed the opportunity to do so because you were occupying their roster.

Term

A term will always have to be agreed to. Terms in label contracts usually consist of a one year period, with the option to extend for a period up to, at most times, 7 years. The label, or an artist, usually require the artist to deliver at least a certain number of songs to them a year.

Exclusivity

Every label contract includes a provision saying that the agreement is 'Exclusive.' This covers two areas. One covers signing restrictions, keeping the artist or label owner from signing to anyone else within the term, and the other is territory.

Under the signing restriction clause, it means that you can't sign, work for, work with, assist, collaborate, etc. with or for anyone else without the label's consent.

The territory clause means that the signing restriction applies within the entire planet earth. So when you see the term 'exclusive' in your contracts, it means exactly that; and you can't sign with anyone if you are not willing to agree to that.

Work For Hire

A work-for-hire clause indicates that everything the artist write, create, perform, invent, establish, etc. while signed to the label, is owned by the label and no claims lys, granting, seeking and or securing, any interest to the artist, other than what's stated in the contract/agreement.

Cross Collateralization

Cross Collateralization means that the label can recoup all of its owed fees from one album, to another one. In simpler terms, if the artists owes the label monies from the advance and other expenses on one album, then once it recoups its money on another current album, then it can recoup its monies from the previous album - if enough of it is left over on the current album. This is in every label contract.

But here's where the game change: Since the artist's contract is a 360° deal contract, then the label can recoup its money from any other venture the artist divulges in. In addition, it is separate from the deal that the label and artist enters under that term deal.

Promotional and Free Goods

Promotional and or free goods, and or products that artists are not paid a royalty on. These goods and products normally consist of album and or recording giveaways, song give aways, promotional uses of songs and albums, videos, bundled albums and songs, discounted albums, songs, and products.

Products can mean anything from the artists merchandise (like t-shirts, posters, albums, radio spins air play, cups, mugs, hand towels, etc.). The crazy part about this is that sometimes your label may still be getting paid for alot of the promotional and free goods that the artists isn't getting paid on. Their argument is that the artist must prove him or herself; and until him or her do, then its none of their business questioning royalties on promotional and or free goods.

However, your and your artist's contracts should list exactly what it consists of.

Liquidation

Liquidation is when the contract establishes exact dates that the label intends to pay the artist on royalties. Some labels have established certain times of the year that that'll be. Usually its twice a year, but sometimes it can be four times. Whichever time it becomes, the contract should state the specific month and day.

Accounting and objection

The accounting and objection provision in the contract states that after the artist is distributed his or her royalties, then they are granted a specific period of time to object and dispute that the royalties are incorrect. If the artist don't raise the dispute in the required amount of time, then the dispute is forever waived. Usually the dispute period is not longer than a year after the artist receives his or her royalties.

Side Letter Clause

A Side Letter Clause is a provision in the contract/agreement that says if the artist is governed under a contract with a corporation, business, entity, Company or other branch, then he or she will still be liable to the label in his or her individual capacity, pursuant to the terms and conditions within the contract.

This prevents the artist from entering a contract/agreement with the label, and then backing out on it because they are contracted with their own label or other company.

All-In Deal

This clause in the contract/agreement states that all fees and expenses that is accumulated in the making of the artist's album, will be deducted from the artist royalties and or advance.

These fees usually consist of studio, producer, mixing, song-writing, video, etc.

Conduct

Most, but not all contracts have clauses within them regarding the artist's conduct. The label wants to assure that the artist doesn't involve themselves in matters that can cause incarceration and or sudden death. So labels include in contracts that the artist must carry themselves in a way that doesn't have the label investing all of their money into the artist for nothing. This is understandable.

Breach of Contract

Labels will also state in their contracts, consequences of the artist's breach of the agreement. The label wants to be sure that all parties keep their end of the bargain and nothing upsets the plan of them staying focused on the big picture. Therefore, they want the artist to be reminded what will happen should the contract be breached.

Non Partnership

The reason for this clause is that the label doesn't want the artist to get anything twisted. They are not partners in the label's company.

However, they are partners in a similar way, but not per se. Their partnership only extends to their obligation to eachother as stated in the contract/agreement.

Indemnity and Covenant Not To Sue

This clause binds the artist to agree that he or she will not hold the label liable to any of the clauses, provisions, sections, and conditions, in the contract/agreement.

Jurisdiction

This clause binds the label and the artist to the jurisdiction that will oversee any and all disputes that may arise due to the artist and label's disagreements. Usually, the label sets the jurisdiction, state, county and court in which the complaints and disputes that may arise.

Free Will

As in every contract, the artist must agree that he or she has not been forced, threatened, coerced, intimidated, etc. nor under the influences of any controlled substances, alcohols, or medications.

The medications may be medications that will impair the artist's rational thinking.

Privacy

This clause is evident. The label doesn't want the artist running around showing off his or her contract to ANYONE whom is not the artist's CONTRACTED Manager, CONTRACTED

Agent, HIRED Attorney, OR officers of the court. So it includes this clause in its contract.

Control

Almost every artist wants to enters the game doing things their way. They want to dictate their own look, hair style, dress code, album cover artwork, music style, image and etc. However, as sad as it may be, they simply cannot do such unless the label owner agree, which is quite rare. The reason is, the label doesn't want the artist paying more attention to less relevant things than increasing their bottom line. If the artist can prove themselves with hella record sales, then the label usually loosen its grip on the things the artist wants to control.

So until then, the label control all aspects of the artist's image, style, music, creativeness, etc.

Gross and Net receipts

Your contract/agreement will almost always have provisions discussing gross and net receipts. And you should very much know the difference between the two. The amount of money you receive depends on it. Its like knowing how to count.

However, its very simple. Gross Receipts is when the label counts up all the money that you have made as a whole, without them taking out expenses yet. Whereas Net Receipts are monies you are being distributed after the label deducts all expenses that is needed before paying you. So don't get them mixed up. Stay on your game in this area because your label contract/agreement will almost always state what you are being paid, whether its you receiving and being entitled to a gross or net percentage.

Pro Rata

Pro Rata is a term used when the artist's royalties are based on the number of songs on the album, then by the amount of time on each song.

All artists are paid under this premise, and its almost always stated in the contract/agreement.

Life Insurance Policy

Overall, the label receiving back their investments is at best, unpredictable, which could lead to them losing everything that they dump into the artist and his or her image and likeness; and as a safeguard, the label will almost always require the contract to state a clause granting the label the insurable right to take an insurance policy against the artist, to recoup any monies that have not been retrieved when the artist dies.

Technically and Commercially Satisfying

When being signed to a label, you must always meet their delivery requirements. This means that if the contract requires you to make 16 Masters each period, then you have to abide by it. In the end, the label will always have a clause in the contract that states "all music must be technically and commercially satisfying." I'll tell you what each of them mean:

COMMERCIALLY SATISFYING:

This means that the label must meet their satisfaction, no ifs, ands or buts about it.

TECHNICALLY SATISFACTION:

Means that the recording must be of a certain style:

1. Recordings that feature only your recordings (unless authorized to use features, collaborations, etc.);
2. Songs of a minimum playing time;
3. Songs that are not using copyrights or sound infringements;
4. Songs that are not wholly instrumental;
5. Songs that don't just consist of sample instruments; and
6. Songs that do not consist of live recordings as the original song.

These are the type of recordings you as an artist (or your artist), will have to deliver; and it will be spelled out in the label's contract/agreement.

IMPORTANT NOTICE

There's something very important that you should know about contracts. It is those contracts that involves or regards minors. This is very sticky.

Its not as so simple to sign a minor to your label or entertainment company, unless under certain circumstances. One is unless the minor is under the age of 18 with a child. The other is only unless the label or entertainment company files a motion in a court of law, informing the court of its intentions to sign the minor to its label.

When filing a motion in a court of law, the terms of the contract must be divulged, as well as its performance duties, royalties and other compensations. The court will then either approve or disapprove the minor being signed to the label or entertainment company if the terms of the contract meets certain wage and labor laws requirements. This is a touchy area because it regards you to be familiar with wage, labor and other laws.

OTHER IMPORTANT NOTICES

Other things to be very aware of are specific details of matters regarding groups. Group contracts/agreements consists pretty much of a single artist contract being applied against a group of members. The only exception is that everything is done pro rata (more about this later).

A group, prior to signing to a label, should always establish some important things amongst themselves. Those things are as followed:

1. Whose the lead singer;
2. Key Instrumentalists;
3. Main songwriter;
4. Key members;
5. Founder;
6. How votes are carried out and how they are decided;
7. How pay is divided (equal, non equal, etc.);
8. How hiring, firing and recruiting is carried out;

9. What to do in case of death of a member, etc.;

10. What to do in case of non participation by a member;

11. What happens if the group breaks up (who can continue on using the name, image, likeness, etc.;

These important things must be discussed and agreed upon by the entire group as a unit, because a breach by one member could be a breach by the entire group. So make sure these issues are taken care of before they arise.

Well these are some, but not all, of the clauses and provisions that are stated in a contract/agreement. However, there are MANY more clauses that is thought of that are incorporated within as well. The imagining of such clauses are unlimited. But if you are not as well informed to know just about all you'll ever need stated in one, or all you'll ever need to know about one, then pick up my book **"X Marks The Spot."** I have done all the work for you; and I have supplied you with the best contracts that is both fair to your artists, and to the label. Its full of contracts for the record label, producer, songwriter, music publishing, talent management, sponsorship, venue renting, booking artists, employee, independent contractor, managers, etc.

HOW CERTAIN PAYS ARE DETERMINED

When determining pay, every label does things differently, basically, the way they want. Some are extremely greedy while others are fair as you'll ever find. In fact, some labels structures their pay in their contracts so harsh towards the artist, that the artist basically have to sell multi millions of records to start seeing any money. Thus, the artists fake it until they make it.

When I structure my contracts, I structure them in a way that everybody eats. I was raised around men with morals that promoted "everyone looks good, everyone lives good, and everyone is good." From the outside you never could tell who was the boss. That's why my book of contracts "**X MARKS THE SPOT:** the book of entertainment contracts" is a book that has universal contracts listed throughout it.

But meanwhile, Imma walk you through how everyone's pay should be like, at least a minimum of what it should be.

360° deal contracts

Lets talk about 366° contracts foremost: The label's contracts will almost always state that the artist is entitled to 25%-50% of the label's Net Receipts. This is whether the label is involved with the artist's side business or not. The label's argument is that they have made the artist famous or notoriously known, and nobody else should be eating off of the artist if its not them. Therefore, Royalties from all ventures in which the artist is paid will be automatically deducted from what the artist is distributed. This will be stated within the artist's contract/agreement.

Artist Determination

The artist royalties, advances and other pay are determined based on the level of status the artist has reached. In a standard contract/agreement, artist's status' are determined as followed:

1. New Artist: 0-350,000 sales of a song;
2. Mid level Artist: 500,000-7 50,000 sales of a song;
3. Top Level Artist: 850,000-1 million sales of a song; and
4. Superstar Artist: 1 million or more sales of a single song.

ADVANCES:

Advances are monies that the artist receive from the label to finance an album. This fee includes producer fees, studio fees, songwriter fees, mixer fees, features, collabos, videos, etc. Sometimes, there are money left over for the artist to spend on themselves, which at most times are spent as living expenses while until their songs generate money for them. Once the artist sells enough records or songs and the label recoup their fees, then artists will immediately start receiving royalties based on the number of record sales. Below are how artists advances are determined:

1. New Artist: 0-$250,000.
2. Mid Level Artist: $250,000-$400,000.

3. Top Level Artist: $400,000-$650,000. and
4. Superstar Artist: 1 Million Dollars or more.

All of the above is at the label's discretion and an artist can only get one advance per album.

ROYALTIES:

Royalties are determined by the wholesale price of the song or album sold. Industry terms lists this as PPD (published price to dealers).

Each royalty percentage is known as a point. For example, if you were a new artist you would get approx. 10 points (10%) on your PPD album. If the album sold for $10.00 PPD, you would be getting $1.00 off of every album (unless you're the label owner, get it?)

So what you can do is establish everything like this:

1. New Artist: 10% PPD
2. Mid Level Artist: 12% PPD
3. Top Level Artist: 13% PPD
4. Superstar Artist: 14% PPD

ESCALATIONS:

There's also other incentives to allow your artist to take advantage of. This boost their hustling grind and encourages them to meet certain milestones in their careers. It is called Escalations, and it affords the artist to receive more points on their royalty awards, and increases their pay when meeting a certain number of song sales:

1. New Artist receives 1 point when exceeding sales in 'New Artist' bracket;
2. Mid level Artist receives 2 points when exceeding sales in 'Mid level Artist' bracket;
3. Top Level Artist receives 3 points when exceeding sales in 'Top Level' bracket; and
4. Superstar Artist receives 4 points when exceeding sales on 'Superstar' bracket.

FOREIGN ROYALTIES:

To understand foreign royalties, you must first understand foreign territory. If you're a label owner, you wanna take the hottest territories and give your artists the fairest possible return on record and song sales. But some territories are listed differently than others. In this regard, you have two different types. You have 'major territories' and you have 'Rest of the world.'

Your major territories will basically consist of Canada, Germany, France, U.K., Austria, Australia, Italy, Japan, Holland, and Scandinavia.

For these territories, you will state in your contract that your artists are only entitled to 50% lesser on their album or song sales. This is still showing your artists mad love because some label owners deduct 75-80% of their U.S. PPD album or song sales, unjustifiably.

All other territories which doesn't consist of the above countries, are considered "Rest of the World." These territories will pay 6½-9% on the artists album or song sales.

IMPORTANT NOTICE

Under this important notice, another term the artist and label owner must be familiar with is "at source."

At-source assures that label owners and publishing companies alike, pay their artists the same value in U.S. monies, when royalties are earned in foreign countries. So if you are an artist, be sure that this is included in your contract/agreement, in reference to you being paid foreign royalties.

TOUR ROYALTIES:

Tour Royalties are determined a little different than other royalties. However, they closely resemble the covered determinations that we've went over. They are received as followed:

1. New Artist: 25% of the 'pro rata' of the label's net receipts;
2. Mid Level Artist: 30% of the 'pro rata' of the label's net receipts;
3. Top Level Artist: 40% 'pro rata' of the label's net receipts; and
4. Superstar Artist: 50% 'pro rata' of the label's net receipts.

DIGITAL DOWNLOADS:

Digital downloads have become the most common avenue of producing money on album and song sales. It changed the game of how music is sold and purchased. Below are how label owners should pay their artists on digital sales:

1. New Artists receives 8% of the digital wholesale price;
2. Mid Level Artists receives 10% of the digital wholesale price;

3. Top Level Artist receives 15% of the digital wholesale price; and

4. Superstar Artist receives 25% of the digital wholesale price.

RESERVES AGAINST RETURNS:

Reserves against returns are monies that the label withheld from the artist for insurance against copyright infringements, unrecouped advances, sampling infringements, sound infringements, and or any other expenses charged to the artist.

The time period for keeping the artist's money in escrow is usually 18 months; and the fee is usually 25% of the artist's royalties.

These determinations apply only to artists advances, royalties, albums and song sales. Now lets move on to monies entitled to other professionals in the music field.

Producers

Producers usually take a lump sum fee for one, or a number of tracks. Some of them however, will accept a portion down and additionally agree to receive 'Record One' royalties, which is royalties extending all the way back to record one when the label has recouped their fees from the artist.

If this type of agreement occurs, producer royalties are determined at the net rate, NOT gross rate; and they're not paid on anything that the artist isn't paid on.

The fees though, are deducted from the artist's advance, under the 'all-in' deal, which is listed in the artist's contract. They are also guaranteed an advance as well, when and if signed to a label. So lets take a look at some of the determinations in which Producer fees are set, according to song sales:

PRODUCER LEVEL:
1. New Producer: 0-350,000 sales on a song;
2. Mid Level Producer: 500,000-750,000 sales on a song;
3. Top Level Producer: 850,000-1 million sales on a song; and
4. Superstar Producer: 1 million or more sales on a song.

ADVANCES:
1. New producer: $0-$50,000 a year;
2. Mid Level Producer: $50,000-$100,000 a year;
3. Top Level Producer: $100,000-$250,000 a year; and
4. Superstar Producer: $250,000-$500,000 a year.

ROYALTIES:
1. New Producer: 2% PPD on every song;
2. Mid Level Producer: 2½% PPD on every song;
3. Top Level Producer: 3% PPD on every song; and
4. Superstar Producer: 4% PPD on every song.

ESCALATIONS:
1. New Producer receives ½ point when exceeding sales in 'New producer' bracket;
2. Mid Level Producer receives 1 point when exceeding sales in 'Mid Level Producer' bracket;

3. Top Level Producer receives 1½ points when exceeding sales in 'Top Level Producer' bracket; and
4. Superstar Producer receives 2 points when exceeding sales in 'superstar producer' bracket.

FOREIGN ROYALTIES:
1. New Producer receives 1% PPD;
2. Mid Level Producer receives 1½% PPD;
3. Top Level Producer receives 2% PPD; and
4. Superstar Producer receives 2½% PPD.

DIGITAL DOWNLOADS:
1. New Producer receives ¼% of the digital wholesale price on each song;
2. Mid Level Producer receives ½% of the digital wholesale price on each song;
3. Top Level Producer receives 1% of the digital wholesale price on each song; and
4. Superstar Producer receives 2% of the digital wholesale price on each song.

RESERVES AGAINST RETURNS:
There is a 25% reserve fee on all producers income on album and song sales; for a period not longer than 18 months.

Mixers

Mixers, also known as music engineers, are usually paid in one lump sum. 99½% of the time they are awarded no royalties. But their fees can be approximated near the numbers below:

1. New Mixer: 0-$2,000 per master or $25,000 per album;
2. Mid Level Mixer: $2,000-$3,000 per master or $30,000 per album;
3. Top Level Mixer: $3,500-$4,000 per master or $35,000 per album; and
4. Superstar Mixer: $4,000-$5,000 per master or $45,000 per album.

Song Writers

Songwriters are other important people that the label will need. Their deals with the label also have terms and sometimes even require the songwriter to deliver previous written songs that has never before been used. Their pay is also determined by a net rate on a pro rata basis. Below is the rate payable to songwriters on a statutory rate basis of 9.1¢:

1. New Songwriters receives 15% of the statutory rate on a single song;
2. Mid Level Songwriters receive 20% of the statutory rate on a single song;
3. Top Level songwriters receives 30% of the statutory rate on a single song; and

4. Superstar Songwriter receives 50% of the statutory rate on a single song;

SONGWRITERS DETERMINATION:

1. New Song Writer: 0-50,000 sales on a single song;
2. Mid Level Song Writer: 100,000-750,000 sales on a single song;
3. Top Level Song Writer: 850,000-1 million sales on a single song; and
4. Superstar Song Writer: 1½ million and more sales on a single song.

ROYALTY DETERMINATIONS:

1. New Song Writer: $25,000 a year;
2. Mid level Song Writer: $50,000 a year;
3. Top Level Song Writer: $75,000 a year; and
4. Super Star Song Writer: $100,000 a year.

ADVANCES:

1. New Song Writer: 10% of new song writer's royalties;
2. Mid Level Song Writer: 10% of mid level song writer's royalties;
3. Top Level Song Writer: 10% of top level song writer's royalties; and
4. Superstar Song Writer: 10% of superstar song writer's royalties.

RESERVES:

There is a 25% reserve fee on all songwriter's income on single song sales; for a period not longer than 18 months.

Recording Industry Determinations

In the music industry sales of albums and singles are certified by the Recording Industry Association of America (RIAA), which is a group of record companies that closely monitors music purchases. The terms they've established are as followed:

1. Bullet: a dot or star that's next to a record's number on the chart; and which means that the record is moving up strongly in chart topping;
2. Gold: 500,000 sales of a record or song;
3. Platinum: when one million or more records or songs have been sold;
4. Double Wood: under 50,000 sales; and
5. Zirconium: under 1,000 sales of a song or album.

Well, you've built your team, now you've familiarized yourself with how to run your label and what is specifically needed stated within the contracts. You're well on your way to becoming a label or artist mogul. Study the game, rehearse to yourself what you've learned so far. Its easier than you think. If you have to, refer back to this book over and over.

CHAPTER V

BOOK YOUR OWN SHOWS/EVENTS

Booking Agents are very busy individuals. They communicate and negotiate with club and venue managers all times of the day and night. But this comes after strategically routing the areas that a given artist will perform In.

Its pretty tough stamina securing dates and venues in both domestic and international territory. Be mindful that the booking agency must also investigate whether or not the venue is suitable to perform in, or if it actually exists.

Apart from this, booking agents negotiate on the talent's behalf. This negotiation is usually by way of a guarantee fee, which is a set minimum; a back end fee, which is no amount up front, but a percentage, depending on what was made on the door; and or a front end and back end fee, which is a set amount up front, and a percentage of the door. These deals are basically determined by how hot the artist is; and the buzz surrounding him or her. Once the deal is finalized, contracts are signed, a deposit is paid to the booking agent, and the itinerary tour routing date of which cities, in which order - is contractly held.

Booking agents generally receive a draw against commissions, from the label or artist, for every venue they successfully book. The draw is usually around $2,500 a month, as a draw against their monthly commissions of approximately 4% on every booking deal. This is because booking agencies are usually regulated by state laws and entertainment Unions.

The booking of acts can take place in various venues, such as clubs, festivals, arenas, theaters, bars, outdoors, colosseums, weddings, parties, etc. Sometimes booking involves other performers as well, also known as supporting acts.

Supporting acts are usually features, opening acts, etc. A supporting act is known in the industry as a "co-bill," and the main act is called the headliner. Below are important things that the booking agent should know and know how to do when booking talent in a variety of venues:

Booking Calls to promoters

For help formulating your booking calls, I recommend you purchase "How to be your own booking agent" by Jeri Goldstein. Her experience is impressing in this field and it gave me great insight of how to convey to you, ways to be successful in booking. Every contact you meet in this field can either make you very successful in the long run, or make you a quitter in the short run. So pay attention.

1. **YOU HAVE TO KNOW SOMETHING ABOUT YOUR VENUE:**

You have to know something about the venue. Research the perimeter area, its neighborhood, what type of patrons it draw, the manager's name, what it charges its patrons at the door, the days it open and hours of operations, capacity, etc.

This is the information that you'll be using in your cold calls. If you don't know any of this info, then use a very creative way to get it. That way you'll be armed with a power response when establishing settlement for the artist's performance. For example, see the following tele call:

PHONE RINGING.
OTHER END PICKS UP: Hello?

YOU: Heyy, I'm Dave Diapoli, a booking agent for Confetti, Inc., a booking promotions and talent management company out of Los Angeles. I would like to speak with the General Manager or person in charge of coordinating the booking of artists.

OTHER END: This is he.

YOU: And your name?

OTHER END: Tony Balken.

YOU: We'll Tony, we're scheduling an itinerary for a domestic tour, for the entire artist roster of Confetti, Inc. The list includes _____, _____, _____, and _____.
And for a favorable discount, we'd like to include a date with this venue.

OTHER END: Sure, what type of price are we talking?

YOU: Well that depends on some basic information like what type of patrons do this venue draw, what patrons are normally charged at the door, and what's the venue's capacity.

Under this type of response, the venue manager or owner can tell the booking agent whatever he or she likes, just to lock the agent in with a date that is to his or her benefit. Then the booking agent would have to conduct an independent investigation to determine if the venue manager or owner was actually providing the truth. However, if the booking agent already knew this information, then its possible, the booking agent could negotiate for a more favorable deal. See below:

OTHER END: Sure, what type of price are we talking?

YOU: Well, we understand that the venue is in an mid crime risk area; and that it draw patrons that are not of a mature crowd. And since it has a normal door charge of $10, with a capacity of 1000 people, we felt that a price of $5,000. is sufficient enough for you to make a huge profit even if you charged a minimum of $20.00 on the night of the artist's performance.

After an agreement of the negotiations the booking agent can then move forward with committing to a date. Normally, the booking agent will need to advise the promoter of providing the agreed upon information to the artists label; and subsequently procure the promoter's contact information, for the purpose of communicating with the promoter up until the day of the show. The process normally worked like this:

1. The promoter usually delivers a small deposit to hold the date, pending an actual commitment, which is deductible of the remaining amount;

2. The date is held while negotiations take place. When all is agreed to, the promoter then delivers an additional fee that equates to ¼ of the overall agreed-to fee;

3. The artist usually delivers a video, internet and radio drop (demonstrations) at the promoters expense, informing the promoter's fan club or venue patrons that the artist have committed to performing at the venue on a certain day or night, at a certain time;

4. Another ¼ is delivered by the promoter, prior to the artist traveling to the promoter's destination, at the promoter's expense, for a meet and greet, for the gathering of photos of the artist, to deliver to print companies to make posters, flyers and other promotional materials; and

5. the final ½ of the agreed upon fee is due on the day of the show (called settlement), prior to the artist performing.

Afterwards, honest and fair dealings of business was conducted, everybody won, and walked away happy. This is where trustworthy relationships are established. When the artist blows up, the label will remember that promoter; and will always be glad to permit the artist to perform at that venue.

Rent Your Own Venues

People ride pass arenas and colosseums on a daily basis. 9 out of 10 of them would never phantom renting one for themselves. On a smaller scale, some of these same people would never even phantom renting a theater. The professional dressed ushers and other officials have scared them away at ever seeing themselves as being so organized.

Renting and securing venues are not as complicated as one may think. Actually, its quite simple. They're mostly owned by city, county, or state governments, or a combination thereof. The first thing to do is to determine the crowd that the artist can possibly draw, then seek out a building with a capacity of such.

The second thing to do is to find out the name of the General Manager. This is the person in charge of the venue and is experienced in overseeing successful events. They will be providing a great service to you, like:

1. A full time staff, such as box office workers, clean up crews, ushers, ticket takers, door men, security, production staff and assistants, their sponsor list, marketing connections, information on ticketing company rebates, securing licenses and permits, etc.;
2. The capacity of the venue;
3. The number of available parking spaces, etc.

Venue rentals are flexible, due to the venue's attempt to attract a variety of concerts, shows, event, etc. a year; and countless promoters shoot for their "all-in" rent deal, which includes everything in 1. above.

Anything else generated from the event besides ticket sales, is called "ancillaries." This usually regards food, beverage, sales, rebates from the ticketing company, parking, etc. So maintain close relations with your venue's general Manager. They can open your eyes to revenues that an experienced promoter knows nothing about.

Another thing. I've known people whom feel that they don't have the right appearance, or is not gifted with the right lingo to deal with professional people such as venue managers. In this case, if you feel too intimidated to deal with these sort of people directly, then pay you a clean professional appearing person, usually an attorney or other professional type character, to secure the venue on your behalf; and close the deal from there.

Overall, securing a venue is alot like booking an artist. You give them a deposit to hold the date; an additional fee for rehearsal time; then prior to the date, or no later than the day of the show, you pay them off in full.

How To Get Around Liquor Licenses

So you're an artist or label owner whom stands to make more money booking the entire venue and having the club owner or General Manager just get the f@#% out of the way. You understand that a packed house means good revenue in liquor sales for the night. But you don't have a liquor license; and bar owners won't lease or rent you theirs because you're too risky, which could result in them losing their licenses. Don't trip, I'll show you a simple short cut around that. All you have to do is price-shop with various caterers, in an effort to use their liquor licenses for the night.

What you'll ultimately do is purchase all of the liquor from them, the caterers, just above wholesale; and then pay the catering employees to serve the alcohol on a hourly rate. All liquor bottles that don't get opened, are taken back by the catering company. So the amount of liquor sold in a packed house has just reaped you lucrative liquor revenue. The caterer has made off with getting paid on the liquor, and for serving the liquor on an hourly rate. Everybody walks away in a win win situation. And the best thing about this all is that you can do this in every city you tour in or visit, if you're renting a venue yourself.

SCHEDULE YOUR OWN TOURING

This chapter teaches you how to schedule and carry out your own touring, whether you're an artist or label owner yourself. Here, we go through key representatives; when and where to tour; promoting the event; and budgeting and launching the tour. Touring is how alot of label owners and artists eat, so pay attention if you enjoy getting full, on all sorts of delicacies.

Key Representatives

Touring is an artist's biggest realization that s*@# just got real! His or her first show on stage before a crowd of fans somehow confirms that he or she is on the right path to success. The crowd's energy and lip synchs fuels the the artist that this is what he or she was ultimately destined to do. But remember, no one person is an Island, and he or she only got this far with the help of a team; so here's where the representatives come into play.

Those representatives, consist of, at a minimum: a booking agent; tour manager; production manager; publicist; and merchandise manager. Let's take a look at what each of them do:

BOOKING AGENT:

Your booking agent are the people or person whom spend a great deal of time on the phone, internet, and or in person, cultivating relationships with talent buyers in clubs, sports bars, arenas, and other venues all over the world. They secure performing dates with these venues on the artist or label's behalf. Their profession is matching talent with certain venues in various genres of talent performances.

A money hungry booking agent can make you filthy rich, while a booking agent with money already, can make you just filthy (and remember, there is no such thing as a good filthy. It represents dirty).

TOURING MANAGER:

Touring manager is another word for road manager. They oversee day to day needs of the artist and the artist's entourage, while communicating frequently with general managers of the venues, about subjects such as sound check; settlement; making sure riders are complied with, etc. They also communicate with hotel staffers, caters, law enforcement for security, medical officials, etc.

In addition to their many job descriptions, they reassure that the artist's hair stylist, wardrobe stylists, barbers, make-up artists, etc. have the artist looking marketable as ever.

PRODUCTION MANAGER:

The production manager handles the technical side of the tour, like overseeing that lights, sound, staging and other technical elements are incorporated into the show. They also oversee other duties, like load-ins, and load-outs, recording of the shows for amateur and documentary footages, etc.

PUBLICIST:

The publicist oversees all press releases regarding the artist, for the sake of building a buzz surrounding the artist and event. These press releases always involve newspaper and magazine articles, radio interviews, commercials, social websites, satellite, etc. anything that tied to a media platform.

MERCHANDISE MANAGER:

This manager oversees all merchadise products bearing the artist's image and likeness while on tour, from t-shirts, music, brochures, hand towels, napkins, photos, etc.; and makes sure that a gross percentage of the merch sales are received.

   These are the 5 most important people you'll need on touring. They make up your touring team; and they should be just as hungry as the artist, when putting in work.

When and Where to Tour

The next things needed to know is when and where to tour. If not strategically planned, the artist or label can suffer a tremendous loss of revenue that it could have otherwised been entitled to, in addition to suffering a total embarrassment and discredit to themselves. Once the key representatives are in place, the tour should be carefully planned. This is 'when and where to tour' comes into play.

   A great deal of this planning has to do with timelines and destiny coordination. The 'timeline' factors deals with single songs and album releases; and how certain cities responds - determined by the numbers from sales. The 'destiny' coordination is determined by those cities that responds in the like.

Social media can also play a huge role amongst the subject by determining the cities that most of your social media fans reside in. However, other artists finds their reasons of touring to promote album sales, build their fan base, and simply to generate money.

As to where to tour, some artists simply base their decisions on performing in the 30 major cities in the United States; and anchor, which means plan around, additional dates around them. This is where new markets can be broke in.

International touring is not yet supported until you, as the artist or label owner, recoups at least enough money to cover the dates. That way, at least if you don't make a profit, you'd have broken new ground; introduced foreign citizens to your music, and have secured new fans to start listening out for your music.

Budgeting

Budgeting the tour is when the need to calculate costs, is better done in advance on paper, than as a loss out of the pockets. You need accurate projections of income and expenses. And everything needs to be included, from rehearsal time, to gas, to purchasing merchandising products, to staff pay.. All expenses are deductable from the artist.

Below is a list of things that you will need to factor into your budget prior to touring, although it is not all:

1. Box Office Fees;
2. Staffing;
3. Permits;

4. Licences;
5. Ground Security;
6. Venue rentals;
7. Opening Acts;
8. Features, Co-Bills, Supporting Acts;
9. Run Arounds;
10. Guides;
11. Press Releases;
12. Print Ads;
13. Marketing;
14. V.I.P. Passes;
15. Ambulance and medical staff;
16. Performance Licenses;
17. Clean-up Expenses;
18. Staff Security;
19. Personnel (box office, ushers, ticket takers, door men, etc.);
20. Transportation Fees (ground);
21. Production Fees;
22. Designing and Building the Show;
23. Tech Rehearsals;
24. Lodging;
25. Meals;

26. Security (road);

27. Radio Ads;

28. Cell Phone Bills;

29. Air travel;

30. Entourage Expenses;

31. etc.

Its a no brainer that club tours are much less expensive than large venue tours. Whichever you decide, please do not rely on "ball park estimates." Be realistic, and exact as possible. Overall, the learning experience itself will be treasurable, and your next event prepares you for perfection.

Promoting the Event

Promoting the event, known in science terminology as "Master Attraction" of your fan base and their friends; and their friends: and their friends....etc. get my drift?

This is advertising and promotions at its finest, tapping into data bases such as internet, print, magazine and newspaper articles, e-marketing, e-blasts, signages, radio, television, satellite, social media, word of mouth, sponsors, DJs, other artists, other events, etc. These are essential factors of a show's success or failure. Announcements, . in which the industry calls marketing campaigns, within these fields are critical. We recommend this within 8 weeks prior to the actual show date. And don't forget to push flyers, posters, post cards, etc.

Whether you promote a domestic tour or an international one, go all in. Do everything you can think of, even bad publicity is good publicity for the tour.

Launching The Tour

Now that everything is done, goose bumps lines your arms. Because now, its either barbecue or mildew, s*@# or get the F@#% out of the way. But if you got real guts, you'd tell yourself that you've come too far and have spent too much cheddar to say f@#% it. Now is the time to gather your entourage, embrace for a premature success, with in mind that everything that can go wrong ...could. Make a prayer, then execute full speed ahead.

CHAPTER VII

HOW TO BE YOUR OWN PUBLICIST

A publicist Is a person whom contacts and disseminate appropriate promotional materials to every media contact whom will allot space for their clients. They build relationships with these media personnels and work alongside them to utilize their resources of local media, national-distributed magazines, trade papers, radio and satellite air waves, billboards, tv outlets, newspaper columns, websites, etc.

Those utilizations, usually occur by way of interesting, well written, paid press releases, of a particular artist or person, for the purpose of building a buzz and carrying out a successive marketing campaign for that artist.

A good publicist however, is more than just a networker, they're a marvelous story teller whom could deliver in all aspects of press, including print, broadcast, radio and online. Some publicists though, won't represent an artist unless they believe that there is: 1, a story behind the artist; 2, that there is a marketable look of the artist; and 3, that there is a success-driven mindset of the artist.

In any event, don't look for publicists to be cheap. Its because they are basically ghostwriters whom makes an interesting story out of the limited information that they're given about you. Within such story, they find a voice in that you can be heard.

But creating a bio about yourself can be easy. Look at the examples that fb, twitter, Instagram, tagged, myspace, plenty of fish, and all the rest of them. 99½% of them are what people would like to say about themselves. But if you have trouble describing yourself artistically, then consider very much of hiring a professional publicist.

A publicist's priority should be a promotional package, which consists of a bio, a press kit and a photograph. The promotional package is the main marketing tool that should ultimately serve as your representative. It should help publicize the artist's event, and entice the public to be interested enough to capture the audience's attention. The promotional package is so important to the development of the artist's career that it is basically impossible to do so without it.

The bio must be descriptively written, and interesting enough to be unique in its own way. It must not be so common in itself, yet relatable or applaudable, given where the artist has come from. Its editing must be to the point wherein it flows easily onto the page.

The press kit is your performance resume. It too should also be short and straight forward, like places the artist have been; performed; his or her abilities; other talents and etc., all in an attempt to induce the public to support the event.

The photograph, which is called the 'promo photo,' says so much about the artist. Here's a picture that should actually say a thousand words. It must make many visual statements. To pull this off, I recommend a photographer who specializes in promotional photos. No other photographer can pull this off, not a wedding photographer, not a amateur photographer, portrait photographer, etc.

Promo photographers knows framing, backgrounds, lighting, colors, coordination of attires, locations, hair, make-up, and story-telling with camera lenses.

Together, a good professional publicist is very experienced in each of these areas, from working with the right photographer, to laying out the most intriguing press releases. This is essential to the artist's career; and it'll evolve as the artist grows to stardom. Before long, a nice biography or autobiography will be the subject of the artist's life and accomplishments.

SELLING YOUR OWN MERCHANDISE

Merchandise, referred to as 'merchs,' is another revenue stream that artists and label owners actually depend and rely on. This is because it itself, could rake in millions of dollars both on and off tour.

The basis of it, is simply selling the artist's image, in the form of t-shirts, posters, photos, coffee mugs, hats, jackets, key chains, cds, VHS tapes, videos, footages, sweaters, hoodies, hand towels, note pads, book bags, back packs, etc.; and the artist gets a nice chunk of this change under what is called a 'merch deal,' which can produce advances, royalties, net sales, etc. The more hotter and marketable the artist, the more he or she can command.

Usually, a merchandising company invests in the artist's image, with permission of the label. A deal is then negotiated that the label will receive a percentage of the "gross" sales after touring, usually about 60% after the merchandising company has recouped its prepaid expenses; or about 70% if the artist is a headliner while on tour. The 'Gross' sales comes also after hall fees to the venue, which is fees permitting the merchandise to be sold on the venue's premises. The artist is paid by the label, a net percentage of the 'gross' sales paid to the label.

The label can also negotiate with merchandising companies, whom can sometimes be retail stores, for favorable monetary incentives, when the company orders too much merchandising products and gets stuck with it. This can result in the label winning in 3 ways: 1, the label gets paid an lesser amount of money, but still receives gains; 2, his fans are the ones whom have purchased these products; and 3, the label gets the remaining products and gets to give them away, gaining more fans.

But sometimes, the label has its own merchandising company, which is a smart idea, that it specifically deals with. So to you label owners, pay close attention to this area particularly. It holds lucrative money for you and your artist.

Foreign royalties and compensations exist on 'merch' sales as well, though they may be basically half of the U.S. percentage rate in some countries. Some countries however, would reap more than the U.S. rate.

Terms governing a 'merch' company handling your 'merch' sales can be negotiated for the duration of an artist's tour. This prevents the merchandiser from getting stiffed with products after just one show. But don't trip, because it makes more money for the artist and the label; and affords the artist broader notoriety. Another benefit is that even though you can't allow the sell of any of your merchandise within two miles of the event's site, within 48 hours prior to the show, the artist, with the label's permission, will still have creative control as to designs, artwork, photos, drawings, layouts, quality, etc. of the images the merchandiser attaches to the products.

Sometimes however, depending on the hugeness of the show, the label will have many merchandisers working together from different venues, in an effort to maximize the revenue that can be made from the merchandise itself. This usually though, is when sponsorship deals has taken place (more about them later).

A clause in the contract between the label and the merchandiser will always spell out a "sell-off Rights" clause, Granting the merchandiser the rights to sell off any remaining merchandise when nearing the end of the tour. One way the merchandiser may want to do so, is through retail outlets.

Under the 'sell-off Rights' clause, the label should have language like:

1. Near the end of the tour, the label shall have the right to buy the remaining merchandise at the cost paid by the merchandiser;
2. That the merchandiser can, in NO WAY, shape form or fashion, stockpile the artist's merchandising name, image or likeness, more than has been ever printed during the course of the tour; and
3. That the merchandiser cannot, in ANY shape, form or fashion, dump the merchandise for under what was paid out of their pockets.

Everything else should be crystal clear within the contract, and it shall have no language stating the contrary.

CHAPTER IX

SHOOT YOUR OWN MUSIC VIDEOS

In 1981, MTV was the first television station in the United States to start music videos. Well actually, there was a disruptive video station on channel 10 that pushed out fuzzy rap videos in 1985, that was overtoned with static. People were able to call in and make a request for videos to be shown by giving the number of the video. The station was located in Miami, Florida and the name of it was called "The Video Juke Box," also known as 'The Box.' With gold metal antennas, people were able to fix the picture and mum the sound just enough to clearly make out the words and images that the channel known as 10, pushed through. You witnessed before your eyes, when the videos was being requested as the number of the video came across the tv screen in real time, though computers wasn't popular. Everything ran through a box that sat atop of whatever television you had.

But videos had already been around way before MTV. It was around in Europe in the 1960s; on scopitone in the 1950s; and on 16mm film in the 1940s. Today however, they're called promotional videos; and they're usually paid for by record companies to promote sales of an artist's music.

In the instances of when the artist is independent, the videos are paid for by the artist themselves.

There are currently no monetary profits in shooting videos, because the viewing of them are mostly promotional. Profits come in the form of credibility and notoriety. Some labels are not even obligated to make videos for their artists' songs, because structured contracts leaves the labels with the sole discretion to do so. However, the biggest the artist become, the more he or she can negotiate on the label doing so.

But every label should make at least 4 videos for each of their artist's albums. But ultimately, the final decision rests with the label.

If labels do make an album, 10 out of 10 of the times, they're going to exercise control and exploitation. This is because they'll be making sure that the video is marketable in their opinion; and that they'll be personally able to exploit every opportunity available, in seeking to recoup their money back. Oh and don't worry, it'll all be stated in the contract.

The videos will always be given a budget; and it'll always be recouped against the artist's future earned monies, including sometimes, advances. In the label's contract, it's termed under "all-in" video costs.

Today, the costs of making videos has dropped tremendously. With so much digital equipment available today, making a video is simple; and inexpensive. You can produce good quality videos with the cheapest camera phones, if shot in the right locations, in the right angles, in the right light, with the right coordination of colored attire. But before doing any of this, you must get the label's total approval; or the video becomes the property of the label, according to contract terms.

From the evolution of videos on U-tube, uploaded clips on fb, twitter, instagram, etc., it seems as if anyone is smart enough to operate hand held camera phones, to carry out the objective of video making. But as stated earlier, get permission from your label. They'll almost always grant your request because it saves them out of pocket money. Who knows, they may also want to get involved in the process.

To shoot videos however, requires only a cell phone and a good editor. Please, whatever you do, don't shoot a video that has nothing to do with the song. There's countless video producers that have done this. To me, its a waste of good lyrics, that don't coincide with the ultimate picture.

SECURING ENTERTAINMENT VISAS FOR YOUR ARTISTS

Applications for non Immigrant Visas are visas that are needed for those label owners whom have artists that's citizens in other countries. To secure visas for them to come into the United States is a simple process. The first step is that the immigrant must have a passport that is valid for the period that the artist wants to remain in the U.S. The place of application for the visa must be applied for at the consular's office having jurisdiction over the immigrant's place of residence. The artist must personally appear there and be interviewed by a consular officer, whom shall determine on the basis of the applicant's representation, the visa application and other relevant documentations, like:

1. The proper non immigrant classification, if any, of the immigrant; and
2. The immigrant's eligibility to receive a visa. Waivers of personal appearance by consular officers may be concluded in the case of any immigrant whom the consular officer concludes, presents no national security concerns requiring an interview; and who:
    1. Is a child under 14 years of age; and
    2. Is a person over 79 years of age.

Additional requirements and information are needed as part of the application, such as applicants whom are required to appear for a personal interview must provide a biometric, which will serve to authenticate identity, and additionally verify the accuracy and truthfulness of the statements in the application at the time of interview.

Other supporting documents and evidence presented by the immigrant shall be considered by the consular officer, along with:

1. Police Certificates, which are certification by the police or other appropriate authorities stating what, if anything, their records show concerning the immigrant;
2. A credible document bearing the immigrant's fingerprint; and
3. A photograph, of reasonable likeness. Which shall be 1½ by 1½ inches in size, unmounted, and showing a full, front face view of the applicant against a light background. The applicant must sign his or her full name on the reverse side of the photos.

The type of visa you want your foreign artist to request is a "B2" visa. Under this type of visa, the artist can stay in the United States for up to 6 months on both business and pleasure. If for some reason the artist gets pregnant, or Impregnate another, the foreign artist can immediately reapply when their time is up, for a I-130 visa, then move to apply for full U.S. citizenship.

The I-130 visa Is known as an "immediate Relative petition," and no one wants this to be commonly known, for fear that immigrants would make bogus excuses to visit the U.S.

and then intentionally commit an act that can cause them to move for full citizenship.

As it regards U.S. citizens traveling to foreign countries, each country has its own immigrations regulations, although some is more relaxed than others. It Is highly suggested that when touring, you make advanced plans, In enough time allowing the application to be reviewed.

U.S. artists entering other countries however, will at most times need work permits If they are performing before a crowd that has been charged a fee to watch them perform.

And before you negotiate any fees as a result of the foreign artist's performance, be sure to check the currency exchange rates and choose the strongest dollar to be paid in. If the foreign dollar Is weaker than the U.S. dollar, then request to be paid in the U.S. dollar. If the foreign dollar is stronger, than request to be paid in the foreign dollar, this is called "per diem."

And last but not least, before all foreign artists depart from the United States, usually when their visas has expired, they have to fill out a Form I-94 Departure of Record, document at any U.S. embassy. This document informs the United States that the immigrant has abided by all terms within the granting of their U.S. visas, and as soon as the immigrant touches back down on his or her foreign soil, then they are almost always approved for any future visa filings.

NEGOTIATE YOUR OWN FILM, SIT COM, REALITY SHOW, COMMERCIAL, & SOUNDTRACK ALBUM DEALS

This chapter exhumes networking and negotiating at its fullest potential. But to be able to, you must have all the necessary knowledge to equip you when this sort of opportunity arise.

There's nothing ever to be intimidated about when meeting occurs of another mind. You have something I want and I have something you want. The objective is for the two of us to walk away, satisfied that we've both come to a content decision with whatever we agreed upon. So whether you're an artist or an label owner, this chapter was written with the intent to arm you with the terms and languages in the main departments regarding the titled subject.

First, lets start with motion pictures (film), sit coms, reality tv, and commercial soundtrack album deals.

MOTION PICTURES:

Film organizers, from producers, directors, etc. work on a time line schedule, with millions at stake.

Clearing and incorporating music into a motion picture is a talent of its own.

There's two types of music rights when it regards film. One is called "acquisition of rights" for the movie, which regards the songwriter, producer, label and publisher. The other is called "license of rights" from movie owners, to others. This regards the movie and distribution company; and possibly a publishing administration deal.

Everything escalates to another level if the artist is also performing in the same shows that his or her music is being played in.

Fees

The normal course of compensation for an artist providing music for a motion picture, sit com, reality tv, commercial, etc., in addition to performing in one, is almost always a flat fee. The fee can vary anywhere from 5.k to 1 million dollars, depending on the status of the artist. Film companies and labels alike, usually appraise these status' as followed below:

1. Minor Artist - $5,000-$50,000;
2. Mid Level Artist - $75,000-$150,000;
3. Top Level Artist - $250,000-$500,000; and
4. Superstar Artist - $600,000-1 million or more. Others are entitled to fees regarding the song as well. Titles of occupations like featured instrumentalists, producer fees, writer fees, publishing fees, etc.

Whatever you do, if you are not a label owner, PLEASE DO NOT ATTEMPT to negotiate with the film company yourself. Have the film company talk directly to the label head. You may however, be able to do so if you are your own artist.

But this is a very fine line that can cause you to breach your contract with your label.

Credits

Another thing to know about music in film, sit com, reality tv, or commercials is "credits." Your label should be in charge of these negotiations as well, unless, as I've said earlier, if you're your own artist.

'Credits' is when the artist and or label is being acknowledged on screen, before the picture comes on, and when the picture goes off. So there's a few lingos that you will need to know while recognizing certain names that rolls in the beginning and end of the screen:

CRAWLS:

'Crawls' are those credits that are shown rolling at the end of the film, tv, sit com, reality show, etc., of everybody's name and role. The label should make extra sure that the artist's name in the 'crawl' is no less prominent than any other actor's name, both in size and placement within.

MAIN TITLE SONG:

This is the song at the beginning of the film, which is credited along with the names of the writer, producer, director, etc.

SINGLE CARD CREDIT:

This is when no other credit is on the screen at the same time as the artist's; or at least, is only shared with one other songwriter. Usually, music producers, song writers and the label are the only ones, if any, to share in this credit. The credit size should always be the same size as the film producers, directors, and writers.

SCORE (OR UNDERSCORE):

This is background music underneath dialogue, action, etc.

KICKERS:

This is when the film, sit com, reality show, commercial, etc. exceeds or draws a certain amount of monies and or viewers. The artist can also get 'kickers' in label deals, called 'escalations.'

PAY OR PLAY:

This is a provision that pays the artist a guaranteed fee, whether the film company usually agree to use the artist's music or performance or not. This is after negotiations have been agreed upon to use the music.

SEQUELS:

A series of movies; and songs being made for every one following the previous one.

TRAILERS:

Short previews before a film actually comes on. Coming attractions.

BILLING BLOCK:

Paid ads promoting the film. Usually those box of credits at the bottom of the movie ads.

TRADE ADS:

Entertainment publication ads.

DELIVERY DATE:

The date the music is delivered to the motion picture company.

EXCLUSIVITY:

First and only of one company during the term of the agreement/deal.

TERM:

Time period of the agreement.

NON EXCLUSIVE:

This is when the label has the rights to license its artist's music to more than one motion picture company.

SPOTTING:

When the composer and director sits down with a final cut of the film and determine precisely which 'spots' need music; as well as the exact length of each piece needed, usually measured in tenths of seconds.

FINAL CUT (FINAL ASSEMBLY):

The digital edited film.

HOLD BACK PERIOD:

A time frame wherein the artist is prohibited from releasing the song on his album, if at all.

CERTIFICATE OF AUTHORSHIP (COA):

A one page document confirming deal points, and reiterating that it owns everything; and or that everything is conducted as a work for hire.

Commercials

For commercials, a song can get anywhere from $50,000, to $250,000 for one year of national usage in the U.S. on television. Major hits can go even higher. Artists, producers, and song writers, get a flat fee. And if they're big enough, then the label can bargain for royalties as well.

Often than not, the record label ultimately owns the Masters to the song. It is the label itself whom license the Masters to the film company. Under the finished deal, the label will have relinquished the non-record rights to use the song, while retaining the phonograph (music) rights.

But the record label wants certain guarantees, such as, a fee plus royalties; a guaranteed release of the film with the music incorporated within; advertising, marketing and promotions of the movie with the song's use in it, and supporting movie clips of the film to use in the label's video with the song.

Because of this, the record company has two interests in licensing its Masters:

1. Is the fee to synchronize the Master in the film; and
2. If the Master is going on a soundtrack album, then what's their royalties.

The fee varies, depending on the hit of the song, the status of the artist, and how its used within the film. The royalties are based on the same, but are guaranteed a minimum of 15% pro rata. The film company will also have to procure the right to use the musical composition of the song, from the publisher.

So now you're equipped with the basic knowledge of musical film rights. No longer can you walk into a room and have film executives talking over your head. Use the knowledge to have your music placed in pre-released and unfinished films. This is additional money for the label, or the artist, if he or she is independent.

HOW TO BE YOUR OWN PUBLISHER

There's big money in publishing, big, big money. It is one of the only sources of income that'll never stop flowing in. It will even keep flowing, 'eons' from now, because someone is always looking into the past, wanting to know about it, or a certain era of it. And someone is definitely always trying to compare, combine and or coincide it with the future. . . . and vise versa. As the quote goes: 'men have two agendas that eats at his heart and soul. One is the fascination to travel backwards into the past; and the other is to travel eternally into the future. With that, comes the tampering and exploitation of everything." Oh how true that is.

But self-published authors have to be ready to wear many hats when pocketing this kind of money. From brutal editor to budget-conscious publisher. They must hire or master the topics of: copy editors, designers, indexers to prepare text to compete on shelves, market and promote, invest a significant sum of money upfront, submit an digital and 'e' format, distribution, shipping, etc.

Though it has its obstacles, the self-publishing world is intriguing. There's much to love about how the self-publishing model works, that it enables more content to reach more customers and that it offers a great deal of flexible total control in the process. Here, we'll touch on various aspects of publishing to familiarize you while making your final decision/determination on whether or not you have the stamina for self-publishing. And no, this is not everything you need to know about the different forms of publishing that is touched upon, but a great deal of the essential basics.

Music Publishing

Music Publishing is time consuming, but super lucrative. Independent music publishers are given a term called 'Vast-pocket Publishers,' which refers to one person. In music publishing, what happens is that a songwriter assigns 100% of their copyrights to a publisher, which takes care of re-registering the copyrights; issuing licenses to artists and sometimes, other publishing companies call 'administrators'; getting songs recorded, also known as 'plugging'; collecting money and paying the writers.

You don't need a large staff to call yourself a music publisher; and there's no need for the expensive distribution network, warehouses, inventory, etc., given the fact that you're now dealing with 'intangible' property. So, follow me as I walk you through the various types of publishing, that earns lucrative income after lucrative income.

Mechanical Royalties

The majority income of song publishing comes from 'mechanical royalties' and performance fees. 'mechanical royalties' are monies paid by a record company for the right to use a song in records. The publisher issues them a license that says, for every record manufactured, distributed and downloaded, the record company must pay a fee within the statutory rate of guidelines set by the copyright royalty board. The rate can either be at the full statutory rate, or it could be at a reduced percentage of that statutory rate, called a 'rate.'

Publishing companies usually asks for no more than 75% of that rate for 'Mid-priced records' and a 50% -66.66% rate for budget records. 'Mid-price records' is 65% - 80% of the price for newly released top line records. Top line is hit artists. 'Budget records' is less than 65% of the top line price; and in some instances, everything under 80% of the top-line price is a budget record.

'Vast-Pocket publishers,' which again, is independent publishers, gets paid at most times, 4 times a year, at the end of each month. For example: March 31, June 30, September 30, and December 31.

Statutory Rate Per Song (per mechanical royalties)

The statutory rate for a song 5 minutes or less is 9.1¢ If its over 5 minutes, by even a second, but not over 6 minutes, then its 10.5¢. If its over 6 minutes but not less than 7 then its 12.25¢. Its further multiplied by 1.75¢ for every minute thereafter.

Music labels never permit their artist to do songs more than 5 minutes, unless the excess minutes are free. Superstar writers sometimes get 100% of the statutory rate; while mid-level writers gets 75% of the statutory rates; and new writers gets 50% of the statutory rate. This isn't always a guarantee, and sometimes the statutory percentage can be negotiated far below what I just stated.

A publisher however, should always limit the composition to the minimum statutory rate, meaning that all compositions are treated if they were 5 minutes or less in duration, regardless of the actual playing time. So in essence, a writer is only paid 9.1¢ if they receive 100% of the statutory rate, or 6.8¢, which is 75% of the 9.1¢, if they have a 75% statutory rate.

Performance Publishing Income

Now lets look into the performance publishing income, known as "performance rights income." Each user needs the publisher's permission or consent to play the songs on the radio, on television, in night clubs, in amusement parks, live concerts, etc.

So how would each user get an individual license? They don't, they secure "blanket licenses" from "performing Rights Societies."

PERFORMING RIGHTS SOCIETIES:

Performing rights societies are societies whom have been granted permission to collect royalties on the artist's or label's publishing. They in-turn, license the performing rights to any and everyone whom may want to use them, then collect fees on their behalf. When the fees are collected, the performing rights societies divides them between themselves and the publisher; and ultimately send the publisher their share.

The most famous performing rights societies in the United States is the "American Society of Composers, Authors and Publishers," also known as ASCAP. In addition to Broadcast Music, Incorporated," known as BMI.

BLANKET LICENSES:

The societies gives each music user a license that covers all of the compositions they represent called a 'blanket license,' in exchange for a yearly fee that can range from a few hundred dollars for a small nightclub, to multi millions of dollars for television networks.

Writers also sign with the societies and are paid specifically by them directly. However, they can only sign with one or the other; and they must own their copyrights to do so. The two agencies also secure foreign royalties on publishing and sub-publishing as well, in addition to foreign mechanicals and digital downloads.

Visit their websites at www.ascap.com and www.bmi.com and read in dept of their rules, regulations and requirements, prior to registering.

Other Publishing Income

There's also other forms of income for publishers to retrieve, like print money, synchronization, digital and foreign monies. Lets walk into each of them:

Print Music

Print music revenues come from "sheet music," which is printed music of either a single song; folios, which is a collection of songs; mixed folios, which is a collection of songs by a number of different artists; and matching folios, which is folios with a certain album artwork on the cover, and various posed candid shots of the artist inside.

Synchronization And Transcription Licenses

Synchronization licenses, known as 'synch' is a license to use music with the flow of visual images called 'time-synchronization.' It includes television commercials, home video devices, motion pictures, etc. The fees vary with the usage and importance of the song, including whether or not its a hit.

Radio commercial licenses are somewhat different, they're called transcription licenses and are paid to the publisher by performance rights societies.

Foreign Subpublishing

We call 'foreign publishing' subpublishing because domestic publishers will need someone to collect royalties in each foreign territory on their behalf. Most countries have a 'mechanical rights' collection organization, mostly government owned, that license all musical compositions used by any record company in that territory. The society collects 'foreign mechanical royalties' from the record companies and others; and then send the money to the appropriate publishers, usually within a 6 month period.

Foreign mechanical license are not issued on a per song basis outside of the U.S. and Canada. Rather, the entire record is licensed for a percentage of the wholesale price, regardless of the number compositions. Each local publisher in the foreign country, will file a claim with their organization saying it owns a particular song. It could be a claim for the entire song, or otherwise a percentage share.

Foreign performances

As with the mechanical rights collection organizations, all foreign territories have a 'performance rights society.' These societies pays the publisher share of performance monies to local subpublishers. They in-turn, pay the writer's share to ASCAP, BMI, etc.

Subpublisher's Fees

Subpublishers retain anywhere from 10% - 50% of the publishing monies earned, with the vast majority of deals being from 15% - 25%, or no more than 50% of the performance monies.

Foreign Printed Music

The foreign subpublisher pays the publishing company 10% - 15% of the marked retail selling price, with the norm being 10% - 12.5%.

Now remember, if this is too much money for you to try and pursue and or keep up with, then you can always hire what is known as a "administrator," and enter an agreement with them to handle said tasks. The largest United States Organization of this sort is 'The Harry Fox Agency,' at www.harryfox.com. The largest Canadian Organization known of this sort, is "The Canadian Musical Reproduction Rights Agency," at www.cmrra.com For other countries, you would have to locate its mechanical rights organizations and determine the best one that suits what you are looking for.

For print and sheet music, you'll have to make your choice with other 'administrators.' Hal Leonard, Alfred, and Music

Sales, are but a few of the Behemoth publishers. It is also very wise to assure that your agreement contracts entered into with 'administrators' have specific language spelled out in it. Language like the following:

Administrator's Publishing Contract/Agreement

The contract/agreement should be tailored around language such as:

1. Publisher's will be paid four times a year, at 60-90 days close of each quarterly month (March, June, September and December);
2. That 'controlled compositions,' which is songs written and performed by the artist, are licensed at 50% for new artists, 60% for Mid-level artists, and 75% for superstar artists, all at the statutory rate;
3. That 'record clubs' or 'budget records' are licensed at 50% of the statutory rate;
4. That 'mechanicals' are paid on all goods, whether they're real or imagined, from all revenue received by the administrator;
5. That 'mechanicals' are paid on particular songs which are used more than once on the same record;
6. That 'mechanicals' are paid on 'public domain arrangements' if a performance society gets paid on them;
7. That 'outside songs' are paid the same fees as contracted 'mechanicals';
8. That 'mechanicals' pays on multiple albums;

9. That 'mechanicals' pays the 'agreed-to statutory' on unlimited songs absent any 'outside song' penalties;
10. That 'mechanicals' pays on 'box set' records;
11. That 'mechanicals' pays on video distribution, video streaming, commercial usages, etc. In addition to its general royalties;
12. That 'mechanicals' pays on digital downloads;
13. That 'single song' sheet music pays 20% of the marked retail price;
14. That 'folios' pay 12.5% of the marked retail price;
15. That royalties are 'pro rated' on the basis of copyrighted royalty bearing works in the folio;
16. That 'print music' pays 15% of retail;
17. That magazines, newspapers, and billboard prints are flat fees;
18. That the agreement term of the life is of this contract is 3 years;
19. That ther's no stock piling, dumping, or distress sales at the end of the term; and the co-publisher can only manufacture enough to meet their reasonably anticipated needs during the term, which must be sold only through normal retail channels, and at normal wholesale prices;
20. That digital print businesses pays 50% of the revenue received from ads;
21. That e-cards pays 8% of the retail price;
22. That digital deals are non-exclusive;

23. That 'synchronization' and 'transcription license' pays 50%;
24. That 'tethered' and 'untethered' downloads; non-interactive streaming, and podcasting shall pay 50% of revenue received;
25. That 'foreign subpublishing' pays 25% of all monies earned;
26. That all foreign monies must be computed 'at source';
27. That translations and or adaptations are approved only at the. real publisher's discretion;
28. That 'synch' licenses must be approved by the real publisher;
29. That advertising, promotions, and other marketing costs shouldn't exceed 20% of gross monies;
30. That advertising, promotions and other costs can't exceed $2,500;
31. That overall administration fees shouldn't exceed 20% of gross monies earned; and
32. That 'cover records' are defined as "a released, single and commercial recording, in the top 5 spot on Billboard, featuring a major artist whom last album was platinum."

It is easy to see that there's mega money in music publishing. When you license a administrator to carry out your publishing duties, they will never inform you that all of these money avenues exist. Therefor, you have to be in the know to negotiate publishing deals. The saying is true, if you knew better, you'd do better ;-)

When your publishing royalties are received, you will have to forward a percentage of those revenues to the writer, and the label. However, if you are the label, then you would only have to forward a percentage to the writer. And if the writer is signed on the label then, its a good chance that he or she is being paid on a set salary; and is not entitled to publishing royalties. You may see how some of these cases work if you look into the rewind of the past at label owners like Suge Knight and Master P. They claimed to be the writers, producers, beat makers, and etc. they did this so that they were being paid all of the publishing royalties as the label and the writer.

Anyway, things get trickier when the label owner tries to be a publisher him or her self. There's certain things that must be abided by and payed attention to. So instead of filling you in on this subject in full detail, I decided to include a publishing contract in **"X MARKS THE SPOT"** as well.

OTHER PUBLISHINGS

There's other publishing knowledge that you should have underneath your thinking cap as well, such as 'hood novels,' magazines, poetry & quotes, screenplays, and pictorials.

I know you're probably asking why, when you're just interested in breaking into the entertainment field. Well the reason is because the word 'entertainment' is broad. The second reason is because each of these subjects I'm about to touch on, could actually be utilized as 'second income' producers to Your label. So be open to learning. You never know, this could be a field you ultimately want to change paths and get on.

Hood Novels and other Book Publishing

When an author deals with a publishing company, he or she is dealing with, at most times, an editor, cover designer, book printer, formatter, and distributor as well. In this position, the author receives basically none of the income from the project that he or she is truly entitled to, And we're not even talking about the publisher marketing and promoting the book.

But when the author self publishes themselves, then all they're in actual need of is a distribution branch. In this way, the self publisher realizes a more higher royalty rate, without the funds going to an unnecessary middle person.

Creating a publishing company and then shopping for a distributor to present your work in a broader and visible range is tremendously better than writing a book and allowing the publisher to edit it, format it, design your cover, market it, promote it, and distribute it. By the time you receive your first royalty check, it'll most likely amount to less time it took you to finish the product and process.

To be a book publisher is simple, if the author can remember essential basics of self publishing. The author should be responsible for all aspects of the publishing proess, or either contract out the services, such as proof reading, indexing, printing, marketing, and promotions, etc.

How about we begin first with the cover design:

COVER DESIGNS....JUDGING A BOOK BY ITS COVER

The cover, as well as the title, can be the No.1 marketing tool for any book. Those factors contribute to having the right package for the right targeted audience.

Size, trim, interior/exterior features and price are also essential; as well as packaging refinement. Choose a title that:

1. Pin Point your message;
2. Describe what the book is about;
3. Is not already taken;
4. Is easy to remember;
5. Sticks in the reader's mind;
6. Coincide with the cover designs; and

Has a subtitle to support the title, if need be, to make the title clearer.

COVER FONTS

Limit the cover fonts to no more than 3 fonts, which conveys a mood of the book. A serif, like Garamond or Times, portrays a more classic feel. Modern sans-serif font, like helvetica, portrays a more classical feel. Decorative fonts are fonts like Comic Sans or Curlz.

One strong image will have more impact than multiple images. However, a image should be chose that coincide with the book's concept. Provide a clean photo that instantly draws the eye in on subject of focus. A good clean photo is one with a sharp resolution of high quality.

Establish a hierarchy of information, making sure the imagery doesn't overpower the title. Match the spines and back cover designs with the font by using the same fonts and colors.

Once the finished product is complete, you can then move to shop for a distributor with the longest reach and clearest visibility. Of course, you'll be instructed to stop personally selling your current self-published editions before the distribution chain put your product in stores.

DISTRIBUTION DEAL

Many aspiring writers dream of getting a book published, and digital printing technology has made self publishing more affordable than ever before. Behind each breakout success, you'll find a dedicated, highly motivated author working on his/her project on a round-the-clock basis; and marketing it aggressively.

What I touched upon in the cover designs, fonts and publishing is just the tip of the iceberg. The money knowledge is knowing how to deal with amazon and other book retailers.... as publishers.

Bottom line is, you can reap lucrative royalties simply by dealing with Amazon and other retailers directly. When this is done, you cut out the middle person, as discussed earlier on. But Amazon and other book retailers won't recognize you as real publishers unless you can speak their knowledge. And that knowledge is based on the questions you initially asks them when contacting them to distribute your book or other publication.

In distributing your book, contact an Amazon, Barnes & Noble, and or Book-a-Million representative. When communicating with them, ask the following questions:

1. You want to introduce yourself as the General Manager of a publishing company, whom is searching for a distributor to sell books through;

2. How are books tracked for accountability;

3. How are foreign sales tracked;
4. What are the publishing company return on domestic sales;
5. What are the publishing company return of foreign sales;
6. When are returns paid, on foreign and domestic sales;
7. Are there any fees associated with depositing royalties directly in the publishing company's checking's account;
8. Who sets the prices of the books;
9. Who sets the shipping and handling prices;
10. Who formats the ebooks;
11. How are ebooks tracked for accountability;
12. What are returns on ebook sales;
13. What are the cost for ebook formatting;
14. What are the cost for print on demand fees;
15. What other costs are charged to the publishing company;
16. What's the term of the book deal;
17. What's the number of books that will be printed up at the end of the term;
18. How are translations and adaptations approved;
19. Are all monies computed 'at-source';
20. What are the circumstances for discounts;
21. What are the extent of those discounts;
22. What are the publishing company's return of discounts;
23. Will any books be stockpiled, dumped or distressed during and or after the term of the contract;

24. Do you have a contract;

Remember, if you don't ask these questions, then they don't believe that you are a real publishing company; and they'll take advantage of your lack of knowledge. But if you do ask them, then they'll respect your company and be as straightforward as the company allows them to be.

Below, I'll get into other publishings as well. And what I discussed earlier about distribution and etc. applies to these as well.

Magazine Publishing

The same outline that applies to book authors, applies in the magazine aspect as well. The only real difference is that you'll need a photographer, photo editor, art director, fashion editor, contributing writer, columnist, newsstand circulator, etc. The reasons for these additional staff, is because magazines, deals mostly with visuals. Beyond the additional help, magazines are less complicated.

Poetry and Quote Publishing

Poetry and Quote publishing is another starved market for lucrative income. But its funny to know that most websites offer these contents viewable free of charge. Its only because they don't have an idea of how to profit from them. After all, they're intellectual property that could very much demand good income.

With so many poetry lovers, poetry could be published to websites, holiday and special occassion cards, magazines, stand-up poetry artists, entertainers, and even movie scripts.

Daily quotes as well could be provided to the same; as well as compiled in books, pamphlets, and etc.

Screenplay Publishing

Screenplays are movie scripts that come in the formats of documentaries, feature length films, sit coms, dramas, commercials, reality shows, etc. Some screenplays however, are gutted for their ideas, dialogue, scene locations, montages, etc. So in essence, no screenplay is a wasted script. There's a huge market in the motion picture field, looking to purchase items of the sort. Start with offering your screenplays for sale, in any, or more of the publications below:

1. The Hollywood Reporter: www.hollywoodreporter.com;
2. Daily & Weekly Variety: www.variety.com;
3. Hollywood Creative Directory: www.hcdonline.com;
4. Fade In: www.fadeinmag.com;
5. Spec Screenplay Sales Directory: www.hollywoodlitsales.com;
6. Producers Guild of America: www.producerguild.com;
7. Writers Guild of America: www.wga.com;
8. Screen Actors Guild: 5757 Willshire Blvd.: Los Angeles, Ca.; 90046;
9. Directors Guild of America: 7920 Sunset Blvd.; Los, Angeles; 90046.

The bigger picture of this is that listing your work could land you a more lucrative job as a writer in a screenwriter circle. Or at the least, provide you an opportunity to present other contemplated ideas that may have arrived in your head.

Pictorial Publishing

Pictorial Publishing is another great source of income. From selling photos to papparazis, to high profile magazine companies like People, US Weekly, OK, etc. and on to news agencies, media outlets, and the likes. It without question, has the potential to produce lucrative income, given the world's fascination with the camera and its captured images.

Unaccountable amounts of social, private and other business websites displays images of photography, capturing and storing entire lifetimes of people and their loved ones in their most sentimental moments. So if taking pictures is your hobby, then why not get paid from it? It'll be like getting paid for something you enjoy doing for free. So, here's a way to publish your photos and retaining control over how they can be used.

Various degrees exist, regarding requiring your permission when someone or company wants to use your photos. The most common and sacred name used is called a 'basic attribution' license. An example of this is when you notice pictures bearing the name of the owner or licensee, like when it says "courtesy of the Ghetti Images."

This type of contribution allows others to use, copy or display your photo and give you attribution for It. It is most likely the only real knowledge that you will ever have to be familiar with when selling, renting and or licensing your photos to others.

Overall, the publishing game is hella lucrative. You just have to have the wisdom to know how to tap into this business field. But I'll tell you the truth, its addictive; and you'll fall in love with the process if you dedicate your sincerity to it.

SECURING YOUR OWN BAR CODES AND ISBN NUMBERS

An 'ISBN' number and or bar code are substituted names for 'UPCs'. A "UPC" is a 12 digit number that appears under the bar codes on many U.S. products. These codes are issued by GS1 US, a non profit group that sets standards for international commerce. Businesses pay to join GS1 US and in exchange it assigns each member its own identification number that appears as the first part of its UPC.

Companies usually need different UPC codes for each product they sell, even if its just a different size. And companies will add more numbers to their GS1 US issued identification code to identify each of their products.

Each UPC can be used to produce a specific barcode that can be printed out and attached to products, or ideally, incorporated into the product design itself so that it is easily scanned at the register.

GS1 US have a first time membership fee of at least $750.00; and then an annual maintenance fee of at least $150.00. The fee depends on the number of unique products you sell, along with your annual revenue.

There are other types of bar codes as well that you should familiarize yourself with and understand. Each of them are essential to tracking the various types of products you intend to later sell. So lets take a look at them so you'll fully understand what they do and what they look like.

UPC (Universal Product Code)

This type of code is a U.S. marker used to identify manufacturers and products sold in supermarkets, convenience and specialty stores.

EAN (European Article Numbering)

These markers are similar to UPS's except that they are used in Europe. A variation of these markers are used as ISBN's on books.

Code Bar

These trackers are used by libraries, blood banks, and air parcel carriers.

Code 39

These markers are used by non retail applications such as manufacturing, inventory, military and health applications requiring numbers and letters in the bar code.

Interleaved 2 of 5

Utilized by non retail applications, such as game tickets, requiring only numbers in the bar code.

Postnet (Postal Numeric Encoding Technique)

Utilized by the U.S. Postal Service to represent a postal code or delivery point code.

ISBN (International Standard Book Number)

Mainly used by those whose products consists majority of books and or other literature.

These are but a few of the codes needed to identify certain products. Below is an image showing how majority of those numbers are designed for use.

This UPC identifies a box of Kellogg's Froot Loops™.

TYPES OF BAR CODES		
Bar Code Name	**Sample Bar Code**	**Primary Market**
Codabar		Libraries, blood banks, and air parcel carriers.
Code 39		Nonretail applications such as manufacturing, inventory, military; and health applications requiring numbers and letters in the bar code.
EAN – European Article Numbering		Similar to UPC, except used in Europe. A variation of EAN is used for ISBNs on books.
Interleaved 2 of 5		Nonretail applications, such as game tickets, requiring only numbers in the bar code.
POSTNET – Postal Numeric Encoding Technique		U.S. Postal Service to represent a postal code or delivery point code.
UPC – Universal Product Code		Supermarkets, convenience, and specialty stores, used to identify manufacturers and products.

SECURING YOUR OWN BAR CODES AND ISBN NUMBERS

As you can see, UPCs and bar codes are essential if you ever plan to do business in your company's name, when a product is involved. Most major retailers generally require product makers to have their own identification numbers; and if you plan to distribute a product then its best to secure your own unique identification number. To do so require you to fill out an online membership form on GS1'a website, at www.gslus.org. Another option is that some internet based companies resell 'UPC' codes at around $100.00 each. One of these companies are buyabarcode.com This allows companies to make money off their codes, and at the same time, prevent companies from joining GS1 themselves. However, you will be paying for the use of that company's identification number, and not your own. That means your products' 'UPC' will begin with another company's registered ID number. It can be a fine solution if you are cash-strapped or working with small or independent retailers, if the retailers don't mind, and are just selling one or two products.

In any event, a 'UPC' is essential; and adds another value to your business if your own bar code is secured.

If your product consist mainly of books and other literature like magazines, postcards, greeting cards, or other reading material, then your best bet is securing an ISBN, which is much more cost effective. An ISBN can be singlely purchased at $125.00 A block of 10 costs $295.00; A block of 100 costs $575.00; and a block of 1000 costs $1,000. This includes the processing fee. Visit isbn.org. It additionally sells bar codes for $25.00 each, separate from the ISBNs. If its a book, usually they require you to upload the book cover.

SOLICIT YOUR OWN SPONSORS

Sponsorship funds are another big market that artists are beginning to tap into. And to succeed, you must ensure that you have a strategic plan backed by marketing research information. In the sponsorship field there are two types of markets:

End Users: which are normally considered regular customers; and

Intermediary Markets: which are organizations that the 'end users' will go through or take advice from, to carry out the event.

There are three groups within those two markets:

1. People who will always attend;
2. People who can be convinced; and
3. People who will never attend.

Every marketing plan must have a media, publicity and evaluation plan, to measure performance, as will reflect your audience profile. The better you know and understand your audience, the more valuable that sponsorship will be to a sponsor. Develop an action list of 3 criterias:

1. Phase the strategies and timeline for each and every strategy;
2. Ensure that each strategy has specific start and stop dates: and

3. Identify who will be responsible for each step of every strategy.

After this, create 4 segments as to why your audience will come out and support your event. Create the segments as followed:

1. See and be seen, ego, elite, bragging rights, in crowd;
2. Excuse to party, social, drinking, group bounding, networking;
3. A possible best performance, best artists, a possible best event; and
4. Glamour, fashion, competitive, vehicle displays.

Sponsors can also often provide non-monetary resources to a project, such as information, time, assistance, advertisement, graphic design, equipment, staff, etc. This is called 'in-kind,' or 'contra' sponsorship. It means providing sponsorship in any other form than cash, like free or reduced travels, free or reduced hotel stay, free help for advertisements of another business, free or reduced radio air play, etc. The possibilities are endless.

If you want to maximize your chances of creating a strong match with a sponsor, it is imperative that you understand what you have to offer. The more precisely you can demonstrate that your audience actively seek out a sponsor's product, the more likely a potential sponsor is likely to be far more interested in listening to what you have to offer.

Make a list of every promotional and marketing opportunity that could possibly be of value. First though, list the 5 different kinds of sales:

1. **New Customer:** Someone who has never been;
2. **Loyal Customer:** Someone who always come;
3. **Incremental:** Someone whom purchase more than they initially planned;
4. **Upselling Customer:** Upgrading to someone with expensive tastes; and
5. **Inbetween:** Someone who plans to spend a minimum.

Afterwards, there's 4 major questions to consider:

1. What portion of your audience does the segment make up?
2. Does this segment influence the attendance or participation of others?
3. What media are likely to appeal to this segment (specific newspapers, columns, radio and television programs, specialty pay channels, magazines, websites, e-zines, etc.? and
4. What message will make the market receptive to attend?

The more 'exclusivity' you grant or propose, the more valuable it is to the sponsor. Next, put together a sponsorship proposal, incorporating the necessities that I have set out below:

MEDIA:

At most times, sponsees embark upon media promotion to achieve their objectives without spending a fortune; and with media outlets whom provide several times their investment in media value. This is to say that you should be receiving substantially more value from the media partner than the funds you invest.

Buying promotional media is part science, part street smart, part creative and alot of common sense. The key to success is to choose the media partners that will deliver the largest portion of your target for the least amount of money.

In order to maximize the media value you achieve for your investment, it Is imperative that you go to your target media with a plan that will achieve your objectives and will create a strong point-of-difference for them and assist them with attracting their audience. If you structure your promotional offer correctly, you are actually doing them a favor, you are helping them to create a strong point of difference and paying their costs to do it. You should never pay more than the rate negotiated for the paid portion of the deal.

ONLINE PROMOS:

Your online presence, and how it is or will be presented, says alot to sponsors about your professionalism. Be sure to get your event listed on complementary websites. Utilize links, familiarize yourself with meta tags, etc.

EMAILS:

Email marketing can be very powerful; or perceived as annoying. An excellent format for this strategy is an e-newsletter. Contact only those whom have permitted you to contact them; or those interested and active in the specific area.

PODCASTING:

Podcasting is a very interesting marketing medium that is only set to grow. With this, you can create content, put it on Itunes, MP3s, spotify, or your own site. And people can download it and listen or watch through some other gadget. You can even change the context, possibly using it for a fund raiser, or let it out for free.

PUBLICITY:

Publicity is the only facet of a marketing plan that is out of your control. Hiring an independent public relations professional is probably a lot less expensive than you think. If you are handling public relations internally, ensure that whoever, handles it as an active member of the public relations community. Be sure your publicist understand what is expected.

In order to get coverage, an event has to be news worthy. Spend some time developing a variety of interesting angles. This will not only increase your potential coverage, but it will also allow you to go to the same media outlets again and again with different stories. And do not discount the value of smaller, more targeted media outlets. They may be more acceptable of your story, and the readers may be more avid.

A sponsor's questions and expectations would always amount to 5 questions:

1. What type of sales
2. To what target markets;
3. During what time frame;
4. From what benchmark; and
5. Determined how;

You need to hold regular meetings with the sponsor, from inception of the contract, right through to the conclusion. Under no circumstances should you have them ill informed.

And everytime you meet, you need to take notes and confirm all actions in writing.

Equivalent Opportunity Costs

If you are seeking money for a sponsorship, you need to understand how a sponsor could spend this money. And to do that is to know how sponsors look at the value that they're trading for their bucks. Like:

1. How many television commercials could they buy in peak viewing;
2. How many black and white pages in the newspapers could they get;
3. How many color pages in mainstream magazines could they obtain;
4. How many weeks, of 30 second spots, at a rate of 30 per week on radio could they secure; and
5. How many billboard spots could they procure.

All of this information is available from media placement companies, but you must be absolutely confident in the value of your offer; as well as the payment dates and methods. So, here are some tips on what types of value that you can offer in exchange for sponsors dollars:

1. Television:
   You should always get at least a 3:1 - 8:1 ratio value for television spots;
2. RADIO:
   You should always get at least a 3:1 - 10:1 ratio value for radio air time;

3. Newspapers:
   You should always get at least a 3:1 - 8:1 ratio value for newspaper ads;

4. Magazines:
   You should always get at least a 2:1 - 5:1 ratio value for magazine placements; and

5. Outdoor Ads:
   You should always get a 2:1 ratio value on all billboard, signages and other outdoor ads.

Always keep a couple of nice benefits up your sleeve, to use during the negotiation process. Some sponsors routinely offers 20-25% less than your asking price. Don't fall for this ploy. You need to remain steadfast in your negotiation, from a position of confidence. Know your value. If they have a problem with the price point, then you need to adjust your package accordingly. Do not ever simply accept a discounted offer. Walk away. The relationship will never get any better. When things settle back down, resume discussions. Inform them that you will rework the offer, taking into account their concerns. Put any defensiveness or acrimony aside and find a way to tell the sponsor that it is clear that you both need to give things a fresh new look.

Oftentimes, a sponsor will want to spread payments over time. You should endeavor to secure a substantial proposition of the fee upfront, both as a measure of good faith, and to begin securing essential necessities with deposits. It may sometimes be more convenient for them to pay the entire amount at once. Or to pay 1/3 upon signing of the agreement, another 1/3 one month later; and the remaining ½ one week prior to the event. But the only way to know which payment option they prefer, is to ask. If your sponsor's end result is more than satisfying, then inquire if they know of any other sponsors that needs a similar commitment.

It is always ideal to meet with a potential sponsor prior to developing a proposal. This enables you to develop a personal relationship with the brand or sponsorship manager. But be sure to do your homework prior to your in-person meeting. It allows you to demonstrate your professionalism and commitment to understanding their needs. If you can't have the meeting in person with the potential sponsor, a telephone interview is definitely the next best thing. And in either circumstance, stick to the agreed schedule. However, some of the things that should be asked in the interview should be geared toward:

1. Has the sponsor ever sponsored a similar property;
2. How long should approval take; and
3. What is the approval procedure for sponsorships.

These three questions alone provide you with in-dept knowledge of how to tailor everything around their approval process. For practice, draft a sponsorship proposal up based on what I have provided you below; and see how you rate.

Sponsorship Proposal

A sponsorship proposal shall contain all of the information provided:

OVERVIEW:

Paint the picture, tantalize the sponsor with both, what your event is about; and how you can benefit the sponsor;

EVENT DETAILS:

List the dates, times, locations, projected attendance, ticket costs, membership Numbers, etc.;

TARGET MARKETS:

Try to be as complete as you can. It should be supported with comprehensive market research information;

MARKETING PLAN:

This outlines exactly how you will be marketing yourself to your target market;

CREATIVE IDEAS FOR LEVERAGE:

This is where you tell them how they can use the sponsorship to achieve their goals;

COMPREHENSIVE LIST OF BENEFITS:

List of benefits that you would provide as part of this offer;

INVESTMENT:

This should list the full total investment, due dates, and any performance incentives, products or promotional support like staff, volunteers, etc. Be sure to include contact details and deadlines for decisions. Draft a proposal that positions each of the proposal headings onto its own page, or at least separates them clearly, keeping it easy and straightforward to read;

CONFIDENTIALITY:

If the proposals includes any of your creative ideas, it should include a legal statement that all concepts included are your property. This should be placed before the body of your proposal, such as at the bottom of your title page.

ex. (c) 2008 <u>Name</u>. All Rights Reserved.
This proposal is copyrighted and confidential; and remains the intellectual property of David Diapoli. No part of it may be reproduced, copied, or discussed, by any means, without the prior expressed permission of David Diapoli.

PRICING:

Never tell the sponsor what you plan on doing with the investment. This undermines your value and indicates your need rather than worth. It also undermines the perception that you are a professional, viable organization whether they participate or not. Be mindful, that it is not unusual for a sponsor to request a breakdown of marketing and promotional expenditure.

CALCULATING THE INVESTMENT:

When calculating your price, you must first understand that a significant chunk of the sponsorship fee will go towards providing the promised benefits; as well as paying for the sale, servicing and administration of the sponsorship. The difference between those costs and the fee is your profit. Once you calculate the total cost of providing the sponsorship, you should factor in your profit, which should be twice the total costs of sponsorship;

PROVIDE AN APPLE OR ORANGE EFFECT:

This approach revolves around the strategy of offering two packages that are completely different from each other. The packages should be priced similarly, but even if they aren't the strategy was wonderful;

EXCLUSIVITY:

The more exclusivity granted, the more value the sponsorship package is;

ONE OR MORE COMPANIES:

It is perfectly alright to have several offers out at a time, as long as the offers differ from each other.

To protect your sponsors from ambush, ensure that no promotional patrons are seen as competing directly or indirectly with them. There are two ways of doing this:

1. Represent within the agreement that you will under no circumstances sell or attempt to sell sponsorship, vending rights, signage, and nor any other ads to any of the sponsor's competitors;

2. Prevent competitor involvement.

If you have taken in everything I've laid out before you, starting with a grain of salt, then you should have learned quite a bit about the music industry and how certain fields within it operates on a level you never phantomed. Nothing is as hard as it seems and if you have to study one chapter at a time until you get it down pact then I encourage you to do so. If structuring contracts is still complicated to you then **"X MARKS THE SPOT"** has all the contracts touching on the chapters I've touched on herein. And if you have any complications of structuring your company, business, label, corporation, etc. then I recommend you pick up my other publication called **"MILLION DOLLAR GAME."** It teaches a basically a-z approach of everything from creating your business to getting instant loans against them, for start-up funding. It also talks about a variety of other informative subjects that you will be equipped with the advantage of having knowledge of. Pick it up.

XV

ETHICS

In the ethical section of 'How to be your own booking agent' by Jeri Goldstein, I'll always remember her one part: "your reputation arrives before you do. It remains long after you're gone; and follows you for the rest of your life." In simpler terms, a shiesty artist or label owner never lasts. In this business, the only thing that matter to folks are loyalty, truthfulness, honesty and doing what you say. Even if it regards a shitty deal that you've entered, and later found it to be unfavorable.

Gratitude is insurance on your career, always incorporate it into doing business, no matter how tired, worn down, worn out, aggravated and or frustrated you are. Treat others as you want or is expected of being treated. Communicate respectfully, clear and effectively. And make sure the world knows, that you are doing good business, even if your appearance or persona tells them different. Make every effort to promote those standards throughout your career.

BEING CREATIVE

Now, we have arrived near the end. If I was a professor I'd provide you an MBA in the music business, depending on how well you've paid attention. Because if you've truly read this book, just once, then you couldn't help but absorb the knowledge it holds.

We are all talented in certain areas that we either have discovered on our own; discovered with the help or hands of others; and or have not yet discovered at all. When your business began to flourish; and your careers are shaped and formed based on that discovery, then enthusiasm takes over. That is the essence of....pursuit.

Being creative is a design, with endless opportunities. Do you know the definition of 'luck?' It is when opportunity meets preparation. If you're ready, you seize upon the opportunity. If you're not, then it passes upon you.

When chasing dreams, never get distracted. Never take your eye off the big picture. Find every thought and everything to be your inspiration, even if its negative. The labor ahead is fun, you're doing something you enjoy doing. Getting paid for it is additional. You're not better than anyone that works for you, assists you, and extends their help. They are the shuttle on your journey. Be patient, be understanding, be realistic, be afraid, be excited, be optimistic. But above all, be thankful and grateful. Amongst this all though, implement creativity. Preach what you practice. Be different. Be successful. Pursuit....the beauty of dream chasing.

BEING YOUR OWN ARTIST

Of course everybody thinks that they can sing, rap, dance and or perform, but sadly of course it is not the case. Alot of artists biggest roadblock however is that they can't get past local success. What's needed is more than the countless hours in a studio, or homemade Youtube videos and social hype pages, because everybody is doing this. What you have to do Is so much more. Then only, will you reach that status you constantly phantom. You want Global recognition as an artist, then look no further than herein and below.

I'm providing the blueprint to raking in money. If you didn't know, you have to first look like money. Next you have to spend like money. Then you have to floss like money. It'll all come back four-fold because money loves to associate and mingle with money. Its the only way to keep vultures out of a circle that caters only to themselves. So apply my teachings. Use them! They really work.

1. Make a CD. Four of them should be club songs, four should be radio songs, and four should be mixed tapes;
2. Send all radio versions out to every radio station in the United States, that you can contact. Send all mixed tapes versions to every underground radio station in the U.S. that you've located and send versions out to all clubs in its genre.

3. Make videos for every song that is not sensitive in nature to being shown on 106 and Park, VH1, MTV and MTV2, and mail the appropriate ones to the appropriate channels. Be sure that some of these videos are shot on speed boats, yahcts, etc.

4. Post clips of these videos on every video website and social page out there. So be sure to establish you a Youtube account, fb, twitter and Instagram page.

5. Publish all 12 songs on every download music site that you can sell your music on. This should provide you some income while marketing you as a upcoming artist at the same time. This also allows people to check to see if you're newsworthy of being heard.

6. Arrange interviews in every industry magazine, such as Rolling Stone, Billboard, Spin, Pollstar, Country Weekly, Hip Hop Weekly, Jet, Ebony, Sister to Sister, Upscale, etc.

7. Now pay attention to this one.

America is quite funny. Its basically the only place that wanna see you walk....then crawl (get it? not crawl before you walk).

U.S. Citizens are hard to please, even when they like something they still complain. They're really not interested in who you are as an up and coming artist unless you're piggybacking off of an artist that is well known and well liked. So here's what you have to do:

    Schedule your first tour for overseas and then come back as a hit artist. Overseas loves any and all things American. They follow American styles and tastes; and even new artists can tour overseas like they're superstar American artists and get mega paid.

So the idea is to tour as superstars from the Americas and rake in a great deal of the overrseas monies, which in some cases are valued as more. When returning back into the U.S., you should be able to continue with the remainder of this blue print. You'll definitely have more than enough money to do so.

Places that holds lucrative money for American tours are the U.K., Europe, Canada, Tokyo, China, Amsterdam, London, Austrailia, Austria, Novascotia, Malaysia, Dominican Republic, etc. These are but just a few. Be sure to do plenty of recording and photo taking while there, to load onto your social pages and other websites.

8. Next you'll have to buy a fleet of exotic cars for you and your artists to floss in.
9. Then visit King of Diamond (K.O.D.) with your entourage and spend about 50 racks.
10. Ball out at the Fountain Bleu before leaving South Beach for the weekend. Be sure to record the event.
11. If you can, stop through Mansions on the way out and floss there as well. Network in all of these places so that people will know who you are when your music hits the streets.
12. Now its time to hit the streets and you wanna hire an entourage of super bad bitc@#*, all of your trusted ni@@#s, personal security and body guards.
13. Rent an exclusive yacht at a marina and throw a party on board. Make sure you record it.

14. Fly out to Vegas and ball out at the MGM and the Bellagio.
15. When you return, rent an expensive Estate home, in addition to two or more helicopters to sit out on the lawn, be sure to arrive in them, and purchase the nicest female bodies to lax around the pool.
16. Hang out on the town with a celebrity.
17. Form a sexual relationship with a celebrity and put out a sex tape. There's many parties whom have a interest in purchasing the tape from you, like Vivid, TMZ, Media Take Out, Kevin Blatt, Perez Hilton, Nik Ritchie, WorldStar, etc.
18. Now its time to get ready for the world because it knows who you are. But it doesn't however, knows if you'll be a one-hit-wonder or someone whom stays shortly. So to kill this assumption, put out a public domain arrangement album, and put it out for free.
19. Do a press release.
20. Tour now in all major U.S. cities.
21. Make it rain in $1s in clubs and other venues; and list your contact information and social pages user names on back.
22. Come back and pay for a feature with every hot artist, then put the tracks out.
23. Travel with a celebrity to a fight, fashion show, event, or on vacation some place.
24. Make movie appearances.
25. Beat JZ's spending plus tips in Scarpetta's, $350.k total. And do so in cash.
26. While out, spend about 100 bandz in Bal Harbor.

Not only would doing all of this make the world know who you are, but they will be dying to get up and close with you on a personal level, the same as they do other artists.

But by now I know you're wondering one thing: Where would any additional money come from to pull all of this off. Worry not, its in here. Just continue reading and soaking up the game.

CHAPTER XVIII

MONEY AVENUES

Of course you are saying to yourself that you need to already be rich to do all of this, or either have access to millions of dollars. However, this is not so the case. I'm about to point out to you all the avenues that provides income in the music industry. But to generate monies through these avenues requires sheer talent and knowledge on the business aspects of things. Now I can help you with the business aspect of things, by providing you this book. But the talent I have no hand in. You have to know you have it, and know when you don't. Below is all the money avenues that provides revenue to a music artist or label owner.

1. Digital downloads;
2. Hard sold products like CDs and merchandise;
3. Streaming on demand;
4. Songwriters income;
5. Publishing income (domestic and foreign);
6. Web Ads;
7. Tours (foreign and domestic);
8. Performance Royalties (domestic and foreign);
9. Features;

10. Transcription Licenses (radio);
11. Mechanical License;
12. Synchronization license;
13. Soundtrack albums;
14. Film royalties;
15. Statutory song rates;
16. Producer royalties;
17. Sponsorship income;
18. Film songwriters deals;
19. etc.

As you can see, money lies everywhere. You just have to know where to pick it up from. And now knowing all of this, do you still think its possible for you not to get rich? Well, it ain't my problem if you don't. Its because you wasn't ever destined to be. So find you a job.

Well, we've now come to the conclusion of this book. Hope that you walk away from it with powerful insight on the music industry and the things other music executives either don't know or won't tell you. But I have given it to you for a simple fee. A fee so simple that people will find every excuse in the world to hate me for writing this book.

Index

Symbols
360° Deal contract 44
360° Rights 29
360° Term 42

A
Accounting 20, 45
Actors equity 22
Administrator 103, 104, 106
Advances 54, 58, 59, 62, 81, 85
Advertising 76, 95, 106
Agent 21, 22, 65, 66, 67, 71, 72, 130
All-in deal 46
Amateur videos 42
American federation of musicians (afm 22
American federation of television and radio artists (aftra 22
American society of composers 100
Anchor 74
Ancillaries 69
A period 30, 43, 60, 63
Artist determination 54
At source 57, 106
Attorney 12, 13, 14, 15, 69
Autobiography 80

B
B2" visa 88
Back end fee 64
Bar code 115, 116, 118

Basic attribution' license 114
Billing block 93
Bio 79
Blanket license 101
Booking 21, 69, 70, 72, 130
Booking agents 64
Booking artists 48
Box set 105
Breach of contract 46
Broadcast music, incorporated 100
Budgeting 71, 74
Bullet 63
Bundled albums 44
Business manager 12, 16, 17, 18, 19, 21, 22

C
Certificate of authorship (coa): 95
Certified cpa 19
Co-bill 65
Collaborations 50
College and radio station 28, 31
Commercially satisfying 50
Commercials 21, 73, 92, 95, 102, 113, 124
Compositions 100, 101, 102, 104
Concerts 21, 22, 35, 69, 100
Conduct 11, 35, 46, 66
Contract/agreement 41, 43, 45, 46, 47, 48, 49, 51, 54, 57
Control 25, 82, 85, 97, 114
Controlled compositions 104
Copyright infringement 58
Copyright royalty board 99

Copyrights 36, 37, 42, 50, 98, 101
Crawls 92
Credits 92, 93
Cross collateralization 44

D
Delivery requirements 50
Deposit 64, 67, 69
Digital download 35
Digital download website 35
Digital format 36
Digitally recorded media 22
Discounted albums, songs, and products 44
Domain names 37
Draw 64, 67

E
Editor 86, 97
End fee 64
End users 119
Entertainers 29, 112
Entertainment visas 87
Entourages 25, 28
Escalations 55, 59, 93
Escrow 58
Exclusive 43, 135
Exploit 30, 85

F
Fb 34
Film business 21

Film companies 91
Final cut 94
Final cut (final assembly) 94
Folios 101, 105
Foreign royalties 56, 57, 82, 101
Foreign subpublishing 102, 106
Front end and back 64

G
Ghostwriter 78
Gold 63, 84
Gross receipts 49
Group contracts 51
Guaranteed fee 93

H
Headliner 65, 81

I
I-94 departure of record 89
I-130 visa 88
Incorporate 130
Independent publishers 99
In-kind 120
Instagram 34, 79, 86, 134
Intermediary markets 119
International touring 74
Isbn 115, 116, 118
Itinerary 64, 66

J
Jurisdiction 47, 87

K
Key representatives 71, 73
Kickers 93

L
Labor laws requirements 51
Lawyers 12, 16
Library of congress 36
Liquidation 45
Liquor license 70
Live recordings 50
Load-ins 72
Load-out 72

M
Main title song 92
Major territories 56
Manager 12, 69, 70, 71, 72, 73, 110, 126
Marketing campaigns 76
Masters 28, 30, 31, 50, 95
Matching folios 101
Mechanical royalties 98, 99, 102
Merchandise 37, 81, 82, 83
Merchandise 81
Merchandise manager 71
Merchandising company 81
Merch deal 81
Merch sales 73
Mid-priced records 99

Million dollar game 28, 37, 129
Mixed folios 101
Mixer 39, 54, 61
Motion pictures 90, 102
Music business 21, 23, 131
Music engineers 61
Music publishing 48, 98, 106
Myspace 40, 79

N
Net receipts 4, 49, 53, 57
Non exclusive 94
Non-interactive streaming 106

O
Objection 4, 45
Office necessities 3, 29, 34
Online promos 122

P
Pay or play 6
Pay or play 93
Per diem 89
Performance duties 51
Performance rights income 100
Personal manager 3, 11, 12, 16, 20, 22
Phonograph (music) rights 95
Pictorial publishing 7, 114
Platinum 63, 106
Plugging 98
Points 55, 56, 60, 95
Press kit 79

Press releases 73, 75, 78, 80, 136
Privacy 4, 13, 47
Producer 38, 39, 46, 48, 58, 59, 60, 91, 92
Producer 5, 29, 38, 59, 60, 139
Producer fees 54
Producers 5, 10, 38, 39, 58, 60, 86, 90, 92, 93, 95, 107, 113
Production manager 5, 71, 72
Products 19, 44, 73, 74, 82, 115, 116, 117, 118, 127, 138
Projection 74
Promo photo 79, 80
Promoters 5, 65, 67, 69
Promotion 13, 121
Promotional 33, 44, 68, 78, 79, 84, 85, 120, 122, 127, 128, 129
Promotional use 44
Promotions 24, 25, 66, 76, 95, 106, 108
Pro rata 51, 57, 61, 96
Pro rata 4, 49, 105
Public domain arrangements 104
Publicist 71, 73, 78, 79, 80, 123
Published price to dealers 55
Publishing fees 91

R
Radio stations 31
Recording industry association of america 63
Recording industry determination 5, 63
Record one' royalties 58
Recoup 30, 44, 50, 54, 85
Recouped 58, 81, 85
Recoups 44, 74
Reserves against returns 5, 58

Reserves against returns 58, 60
Riders 72
Routing 64

S
Sampling infringements 58
Score 6, 93
Score 93
Screen actors guild 22, 113
Secretary 12, 18, 19, 20
Self publishing 108, 110
Sell-off rights 83
Sequels 6, 93
Settlement 66, 68, 72
Sheet music 101, 103, 105
Side person performance 42
Social media 25, 40, 74, 76
Songwriter 39, 48, 52, 61, 62, 91, 92, 98
Songwriter fees 54
Songwriters 3, 5, 39, 61, 63, 138, 139
Songwriters determination: 62
Songwriting 21, 40, 46
Sound check 72
Sound infringement 50, 58
Sponsorship 11, 21, 42, 48, 83, 119, 120, 124, 126, 127, 128, 129
Sponsorship 119, 126, 139
Sponsorship proposal 121
Spotting 7, 94
Statutory rates 99
Stockpile 83

Streaming on demand 42, 138
Studio 29, 38, 40, 46, 133
Studio fees 54
Subpublisher's fees 7, 103
Subpublishing 7, 101, 102, 106
Supporting acts 65, 75

T
Technically and commercially satisfying 50
Term 30, 94, 98, 105, 111
Term deal 44
Territory 43, 56, 64, 102
'Tethered' and 'untethered' downloads 106
Ticket sales 69
Time-synchronization 102
Tour royalties 5, 57
Tours 21, 37, 40, 76, 135
Trade ads 6
Trade ads 94
Trademark 29, 37
Trailer 42
Transcription license 106
Transcription license 7, 102
Transcription licenses 102
Transcription licenses 139
Treasurer 19, 20
Treasurer 3, 12, 19
Twitter 34, 79, 86, 134

U
Underscore 6, 93
Union 22
Unsolicited' material 15
Untethered 106
User name 37, 136
U.S. Rate 82

V
Vast-pocket publisher 98, 99
Venue 48, 64, 65, 66, 67, 68, 69, 70, 76, 81
Venue manager 64
Video juke box 84
Videos 40, 81, 84, 85, 86, 133, 134
Visas 87, 89
Visas 87

W
Webcasting 42
Work-for-hire 43
Writers guild of america 113

X
X marks the spot 107

Y
Youtube 133, 134

Other Books by David Dipoali

Million Dollar Game: The Come Up Strategies For Small Business Start Ups
ISBN number: 978-0-9903853-0-1 (print)
978-0-9903853-1-8 (ebook)
978-0-9903853-2-5 (MOBI)

X Marks The Spot: The Book Of Entertainment Contracts
ISBN number: 978-0-9903853-3-2 (print)
978-0-9903853-4-9 (ebook)
978-0-9903853-2-5 (MOBI)

www.ingramcontent.com/pod-product-compliance
Lightning Source LLC
Chambersburg PA
CBHW070733230426
43665CB00035B/2228